Fast-Folded Flower Quilts and Bags

30 Projects for You and Your Home

Laura Farson

©2004 by Laura Farson

Published by

kp krause publications
An F+W Publications Company

700 East State Street • Iola, WI 54990-0001
715-445-2214 • 888-457-2873
www.krause.com

Our toll-free number to place an order or obtain
a free catalog is (800) 258-0929.

All rights reserved. No portion of this publication may be reproduced or
transmitted in any form or by any means, electronic or mechanical, including
photocopy, recording, or any information storage and retrieval system, without
permission in writing from the publisher, except by a reviewer who may quote
brief passages in a critical article or review to be printed in a magazine or
newspaper, or electronically transmitted on radio or television.

Library of Congress Catalog Number: 2003117115

ISBN: 0-87349-725-2

Edited by Maria L. Turner
Designed by Sharon Laufenberg

Printed in the United States of America

Dedication

To my family, who taught me how to make-do and how to innovate.

Acknowledgments

As its author, I'm part of a team that put this book together. Many people contributed to that end. I would like to thank these people for their generous support: Lisa Shepard, Marcus Brothers; Marci Brier, A & E; John Bowling, Maximum Industries; Sandy Muckenthaler, Hoffman; and Sarah Klein and J. Mackenbrock of Westfalenstoffe. Pfaff provided the sewing machine shown in the photos, and The Warm Company, Olfa, and Prym Dritz supplied the tools.

Instrumental in publishing this book are many at Krause Publications, but specifically: acquisitions editor Julie Stephani, editor Maria Turner, cover designer Marilyn McGrane, and graphic designer Sharon Laufenberg. Without their contributions, it never would have happened.

Lynne Beykirch, besides offering encouragement, read the manuscript and noted corrections. My cheering section included Melania Thompson, Cindy Marshall, and the Folded Frenzies group of the Springfield Quilt Guild.

Dot and James Hackney, Bill and Kyle Schultz, and Jan and Dick Williams graciously allowed photographer Greg Daniels and me to use the spaces inside and outside their homes. I am especially indebted to Greg for photographing this book on his vacation.

Table of Contents

Introduction

The projects you will find within this book are so much fun to look at and just as much fun to make. There are many choices that range from a simple book tote to bed quilts. The designs look really complicated, but are made simple by using a raw-edge bias fabric bending technique first seen in my previous two books: *Fast-Folded Flowers* (Krause Publications, 2001) and *Ragged-Edge Flowers* (Krause Publications, 2002).

These projects have mixed-and-matched flower shapes formed by folded bias fabric edges. By being cut on the bias, they bend easily into curvy shapes. The cut edges fray, creating soft fluffy-textured edges, but they also remain sturdy because they do not unravel.

The basic construction technique is common to all the flower and leaf units. Two fabrics—complementary or contrasting—are cut into a geometric shape. The pieces are matched with the right side out. Corners or points are folded to the center and pressed into another shape; flowers are hexagons, octagons, or dodecagons (don't be frightened; it's really just a sunflower). Leaf units are square or rectangular. They can be central to the design or can simply fill in on the side. These folded "units" are then topstitched around the folds to secure the outer edges. Now for the fun part: The raw edges are bent back and topstitched. These curvy fabric edges reveal the

inner layer of fabric and form either petals or leaves. It's that simple.

To finish: layer, fold, turn back, and topstitch. A batting layer is added to fluff up quilts, and fusible fleece is used to firm up totes and bags. All the stitching is done on the sewing machine, and when you're finished topstitching the petals, you're done. All the layers are combined during the construction, so there's no cumbersome layering of large sheets of batting or backing.

Chapter 1 walks you through all the basics: the tools needed; fabric selection; template-making; simple unit construction; joining the units; and binding. Specific step-by-step instructions for each unit, beginning with the three flowers, are included in the next section. Make some for practice and use them for handy potholders, little mats for flowerpots, or save them for inclusion in a bigger project.

Basic leaves have two "petals" and can be squares or rectangles. They form the backgrounds of flower units, the borders of quilts, and the sides of some bags. Their cousins are "mirror" leaves. These units have four "petals" that reflect along the midline. They, too, are square or rectangular, and appear as borders or backs in the projects.

The "building blocks" are the basic geometric shapes that are either joined in flat groups or "built" into three-dimensional shapes. Triangles combine to become a pyramid by themselves, or can be combined with rectangles to form a "jewel box." Squares are versatile in the treasure box and also combine with octagon flowers to fill in the gaps. Basic rectangles are the same as the leaf blocks in different colors where they fill in and add to other flower and geometric shapes.

The modular square and rectangle units are constructed in the same manner. The only difference is in the basic shape. These units are so fun because they have four layers of fabric, so when the petals are turned back, many secondary shapes are formed. These have tremendous color-study potential with lights and darks, prints and stripes as examples.

The most illusion-producing shape is the diamond. Here, too, the potential for color-study is great. Three shades produce the "tumbling block pattern." Experiment with different colors and shades for special effects.

The remaining section contains the "parts" necessary to complete the projects. In this part of the book, you will find detailed instructions for making the bottom, back, or side pieces, the handles for the bags, and the patches to fill in gaps between joined units.

A major part of this book is devoted to projects. The instructions for projects include the specific information needed to complete its parts. Included are

fabric and notions, the cutting plan, references to any templates, and the steps for assembly. Illustrations and photos show the special details for each project.

The projects range from personal accessories, eyeglass cases, coin and neck pouches, a checkbook cover, a name tag, and a treasure box. These are simple to make and are suggested as the place to begin. The totes are slightly more complex, but very simple to construct. As an example, the Magic Square Tote, page 59, is just two modular squares stitched to a bottom piece. Tack the handles and you're "good to go." Similarly, the Tiny Tote, page 61, is just a leaf flower combination attached to a circular handle. The flowers form inner pockets, and the bag itself closes with simple hook-and-loop tape. The backpack has many steps, but they are quite easy to execute and the result is a fun design with many practical uses.

Most complex of the designs are the bags, primarily because they all have a zipper insertion or an assembly that joins the flower units. Here again, the effort is worth the result. A few more steps than a tote yield a truly authentic handbag. Simplest is the pyramid. Four triangles zip together to make this clever bag, which is perfect for a young girl or an evening out. Slightly roomier and just as quick to make is the jewel box. My all-time favorite is the citrus slice—so simple! One flower unit cut in half with a zipper and tape, and it's done. There are so many color combinations that you'll want to try for a whole fruit bowl. As it turns out, it's a handy size for a few necessities. Lengthen the handle and it can be worn as a shoulder bag.

For the traditionalist, I've included the Grandma's Not-a-Square Bag, page 74. This is an expanded version of the Magic Square Tote. It has a full zipper, more room, and longer handles, so it can be carried as a shoulder bag.

The modular square has many color and fabric possibilities. The hatbox and barrel bags are practical, yet fun and beautiful. Either can be used for travel items or to carry around every day. And although it's one of the smallest bags, the Zippy Tote is quite useful. It has a front pocket hidden under the flower and a spacious zippered inner area that's well-suited for a camera, phone, wallet, and keys.

There are so many fabric and design choices, you can create an entire "wardrobe" of bags.

The household projects range from simple four-flower wall hangings to more complicated quilts.

The easiest to construct are the diamond and rectangular placemats with matching coasters. The bathmats consist of just seven or eight flower units. They can be stacked up in an assembly line and completed lickety-split, as all it takes to join them is a zigzag stitch over the seams.

Most impressive are the quilts. Playing with color and value can create wonderful illusions with the diamond units. Again, once the units are topstitched, they're a cinch to finish with zigzag stitching. Square-on-squares replicate a really complicated pattern with just layered fabric and quilt stitches.

Finally, my favorite and the inspiration for this book is the Garden Plants Quilt. This design makes me want to collect every batik fabric I can find and "plant" a really big garden. There's so much happening in the flowers and leaves and yet it's just two units with patches filling the gaps. Can't you just imagine a spring wedding and this as your gift? You'll notice that I couldn't resist wrapping myself in it for the Final Word, page 114. And this is my final word: Make this quilt and wrap yourself in the garden all year long.

Best wishes for your bouquet of flowers!

Laura
One Quirky Quilter!

1 How to Make the Flowers

B looming flowers are fast, fun, and easy! There are many choices for shapes, techniques, fabrics, and colors. Designs range from simple to complex, but the construction stays easy.

The Basics

The projects within this book have a myriad of flower shapes, formed by folded bias edges of fabric.

The bias-cut fabric is left raw, which when laundered, fluffs up to form dimensional surface texture. These unfinished bias edges bend easily to form the curves of the petal edges. When the quilts are washed and dried, they bloom into fuzzy, lettuce edges.

Edges are all cut on the bias. This is primarily for ease in turning the petal edges, and secondarily, to minimize fraying of the raw edges. Bias causes a fairly even fraying of the raw edges; whereas, straight grain cutting allows threads to shred, which degrades the integrity of the fabric and the seam line.

All components are made by using the same basic construction technique. Two fabrics are cut with a template or ruler into a particular shape with corners or points. These fabric pieces are placed right sides out (wrong sides together), with their edges matching. The corners and/or points are folded and pressed to the center of the shape. The folded edges are then topstitched into dimensional flower petals. These units either are joined to each other or with "patches" cut to fit between the flowers. The term "unit" refers to the layered, folded, and sometimes topstitched packet of fabric and batting (when included).

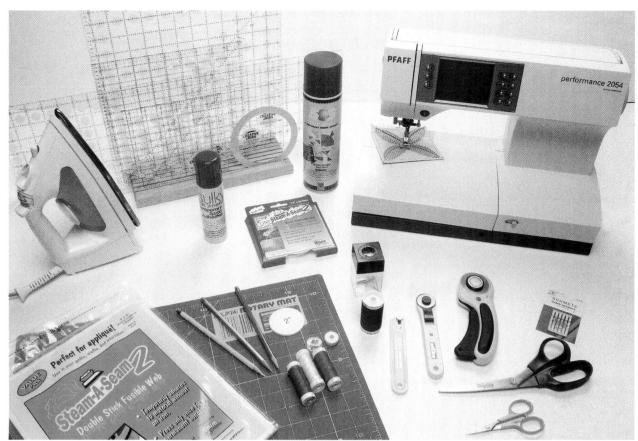

Tools and supplies.

Tools and Supplies

These are the basic tools and supplies needed for construction of the projects:

* Iron
* Silk pins
* Rotary cutter (45mm)
* Rotary point cutter
* Paper and pencils
* Rotary rulers (1" x 12", 12½" square, and 6" x 24")
* Sewing machine needles: "leather" for multiple batik layers and "quilting" 90/14
* Bobbins
* Thread
* Scissors (4")
* Dressmaker shears
* Rotary cutting mat (18" x 24")
* Temporary adhesive spray
* Fray Check™
* Sewing machine
* Walking foot or dual feed feature on sewing machine
* Lint roller

Fabric selection, in terms of choosing what colors to use, plays a significant role in maximizing your design options.

Fabric Selection and Preparation

Blooming flowers are created with bias-cut fabric edges left raw, so fabrics that are yarn-dyed or finely woven are best suited to this technique. Batiks, homespun and yarn-dyed flannels, and brushed woven fabrics are excellent choices. My preference is 100 percent cotton.

Batiks are wonderful for totes and bags because of their artistic beauty, fine thread count, and wonderful colors.

Flannel fabrics vary in weight and texture. Some are yarn-dyed, in which case both the front and back sides are the same color. These are most desirable for areas that are left really ragged.

Quilting cottons can be used for finished parts of modular square and rectangle projects, but are unsuitable for raw-edge areas of a project. It isn't necessary or desirable to launder the fabric, because the unwashed fabric is more stable and easier to handle.

Prepare the fabric by pressing out the major wrinkles. Fold with the selvedges even with one another.

At least two fabric patterns/colors are paired for any given project. One is for the inside and the other for the outside (which also forms the back side of the project).

Most projects utilize the same fabric in several units. Therefore, you may cut more than one layer at a time.

Prepare the fabric by folding selvedge to selvedge. In some cases, the fabric can be folded again, with the fold placed in line with the selvedge, thereby making four layers.

For very long yardage, shorter sections may be cut to ease the handling. Special cutting instructions are specified in the chapter or projects.

The projects use either standard-size rulers for square cutouts or photocopied paper to cut out the fabric shapes. Purchased plastic templates are also available. (See A Final Word, page 114, for ordering information).

For basic units, there are two fabric cutouts: one inside and one for the outside. Each part can be cut individually with the ruler and rotary cutter. The fabric cutouts are layered and the corners are matched. When fleece or batting is inserted, it's best to cut the layers separately to allow placement of the batting between the inner and outer pieces.

When the project doesn't have a filling, the first fabric cutout can be layered onto the second fabric and used as a pattern. Flannel and homespun fabrics are "fuzzy," so the pieces don't shift during the cutting process. Since the fabrics are already matched, there is minimal handling, which, in turn, controls distortion of the bias edges.

Template Construction

The templates in the back of the book are used when creating some of the projects. They provide a simple way for you to know the exact shape(s) needed to make your piece just perfect.

1. Note the number of copies specified on the template pattern in the Appendix.
2. Cut along the solid lines and join as instructed in the diagram.
3. Use the lines on your rotary mat to keep the pieces aligned.

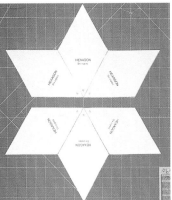

Hexagon template on the rotary mat.

❋ Laura's Hint:

On large projects with many fabric cutouts, replace the template after it becomes tattered.

Cutting Components

When doing the projects in this book and using the paper templates, I suggest using temporary adhesive to make the cutting easier. These sprays are designed to provide a light, sticky surface. They wash out or dissipate after a short period of time.

1. Spray the backside of the paper template with temporary adhesive.
2. Place the template on the folded fabric set with the no-cut edge parallel to the grain line.
3. Cut with ruler and rotary cutter through the two layers.

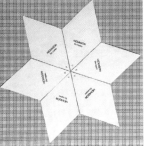

Template rotated on the fabric.

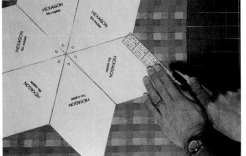

Cutting fabric with a template, ruler, and rotary cutter.

4. For the inner corners of star-shaped pieces, cut with scissors or a rotary point cutter, as shown below.

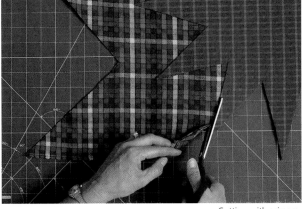

Cutting with scissors.

Cutting with point trimmer.

5. Repeat steps 1 through 4 for the remaining number of pieces needed for the project.

Fusible Fleece or Batting

Fusible fleece is an essential part of the totes and bags, as it provides stiffness. Choose a hefty weight for bags and totes, and a lighter weight for the accessories.

For flower and leaf units, the fleece is placed just in the center area of the unit layered between the inside and outside fabrics and then fused in place.

For quilt projects, a light thin layer of batting works best. Thermore™ by Hobbs is my favorite. A very thin cotton craft weight batting is also fine.

Batting selection.

1. Prepare one of the fleece/batting templates as instructed in the example template, page 119.

2. Place the template on one or more layers of fleece/batting. A slight spritz of adhesive on the back of the template can be helpful, but don't overdo it because it could pull the batting layers apart.

3. Cut the necessary number of fleece/batting pieces, either with a ruler and rotary cutter or with scissors.

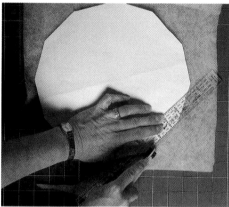

Cutting batting with ruler and rotary cutter.

4. Layer the fleece/batting piece in the center of the fabric cutout between the inner and outer fabric layers. In most cases, it is not necessary to baste or tack the batting as it will be sewn into the unit in a later step. Fuse fleece according to the manufacturer's instructions.

5. Place the inner fabric cutout on top of the batting layer and match the corners. Note: When folded, the points or corners will not be filled with batting.

Batting cut out on sunflower.

6. Layer fusible web between the fabric and fleece. Fuse.

Folding

1. Fold the points/corners to the center and pin in place.

2. Topstitch ½" from the outer folds and stitch a 2" circle in the center of the unit over the points. The 2" circle template is on page 126.

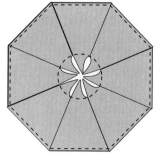

Diagram of topstitching the unit.

Petal Turning

Flower and block units are made by folding layered fabric into geometric shapes. The folded areas are cut on the bias. These bias edges are bent back into curves and topstitched to form the petals and reveal the inner fabric layer.

1. Turn back the fabric layers and stitch along the folded petal flaps to reveal the inner fabric.

2. Start at the point where the center topstitching secures the flap and turn back the bias edges of both layers. The petal naturally bends in a tapered arc. Avoid excessive stretching, as it will distort the unit.

3. Place your stitches either along the cut edge, centered, or along the fold, as desired.

4. Continue along all the petal edges, starting and ending in the center.

5. Between the petals in the center, stitch across the points to flatten them.

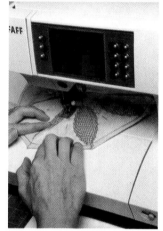

Turn back and topstitch petals.

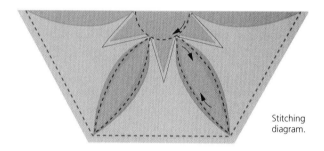

Stitching diagram.

Joining

Squares, rectangles, triangles, diamonds, and hexagons may be joined by butting the pieces close together and zigzag stitching over the seam.

1. Arrange the units in the desired pattern. Butt the sides to be joined and zigzag over the seam.

Join with zigzag stitching.

2. Join two rows of primary pieces with zigzag stitches across the common sides of the units. In the octagon example, the four joined units form a square gap in the center and half-square triangles around the sides.

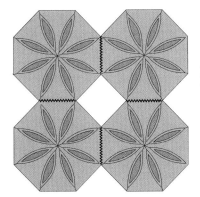

Join octagons with zigzag stitching across the common sides.

3. In the octagons and sunflowers, gaps are noticeable at this stage, but these spaces will be filled with layered fabric patches. The patches are designed to cleverly and securely fill the gaps. Instructions on how to make patches are on pages 30-33.

4. Secure the patches by stitching through all layers as follows:

a. Choose a zigzag or hemstitch on your sewing machine and use its maximum width. Sew a test piece to check the placement of the stitching.

b. Place the patch area of the joined pieces under the presser foot so that the ridge of the primary piece rests under the sewing machine needle.

c. Stitch along the edge of this ridge so that one swing of the zigzag or hemstitch catches the raw edge of the patch and the other stitch pierces the primary piece.

d. Stitch along the remaining sides of the patch and continue across your first stitches to secure the patch.

Hemstitching the patch.

❋ Laura's Hint

Carefully roll up the portion of the section you're not working on to keep it out of the way while sewing the patches.

5. Add edge and corner patches.

Joining with Over-Edge Zigzag Stitch

As an alternative to butting the units, you can over-edge zigzag. This is a more secure seam, but has ridges at the corners.

1. Loosen the tension slightly on your sewing machine (I move my setting from 5 to 3). Set the zigzag stitch width at 5.5mm and the length at 1.5mm.

2. Arrange the units into the desired pattern.

3. Pick up two units that are to be joined and place them right sides together. Place the edges to be joined to the right side.

4. Place two layered units under the needle so that the right side of the stitch falls off the edge of the fabric. The left part of the stitch should pierce all the fabric layers. Back-tack or tie off at the beginning and end of the seam.

Join two hexagons with over-edge zigzag stitch.

5. Stitch along the seam line and back-tack.

6. After completing the seam, open the units so that they lie flat. If the units won't unfold, loosen the tension and stitch position. The stitches should resemble a ladder.

7. Repeat steps 2 through 6 for each of the units in a row.

8. Join the remaining units into rows.

9. Place a pair of rows with right sides together, matching the intersections of the joined units.

10. Stitch the length of the row using the same backstitching and over-edge zigzag technique.

11. Join the pairs of rows to complete the project.

12. Insert and topstitch patches, as on pages 30-33.

Binding

Simple bias-cut strips are joined to make the length needed for the outer edge of a project. The strips are first sewn to the back side, and then wrapped to the front without further turning. Once stitched in place, the raw edges bloom to match the petals when laundered.

Cutting Bias Strips

1. Place the binding fabric on the rotary cutting mat with the selvedge even with the horizontal lines of the mat.

2. Place a long (24") rotary ruler on the fabric so that the 45-degree line is on the selvedge.

3. Cut along the edge of the ruler.

4. Move the ruler so that 1⅛" of fabric is under the edge and cut along the edge of the ruler.

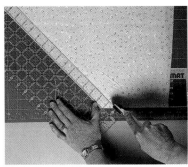

Place the long ruler at a 45-degree angle to cut a bias strip.

For a quilt project:

1. Cut a number of 1⅛" strips (or specified width) of bias binding equal to twice the combined length and width of the project, plus 20 inches. Smaller projects usually require one or two strips as indicated in the cutting plan.

2. Join the binding strips by placing the ends right sides together at a right angle ¼" from the crossed pieces.

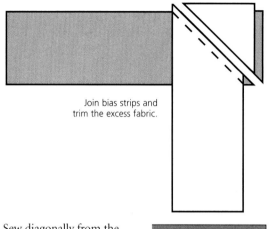

Join bias strips and trim the excess fabric.

3. Sew diagonally from the upper left corner to the lower right corner as shown.

4. Repeat steps 2 and 3 for the remaining strips.

5. Trim the extra fabric at the joint.

6. Press the seams open.

7. With right sides together on the back of the quilt, place the binding strip on the edge of the joined units.

8. Stitch ¼" from the edge, turning the corners with a miter. Keep the strips flat and loose. Do not tug or pull while sewing. Stitch to ¼" from the corner.

1/4"

Stitching line.

Miter

1. At the corner, fold the binding strip at a 45-degree angle. The right side of the binding strip will be facing up.

2. Refold the strip upon itself so that it turns the corner. The binding strip will be face-down on the corner folds.

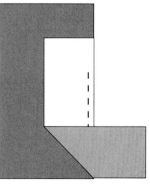

Fold corner.

3. Sew from the corner along the next side.

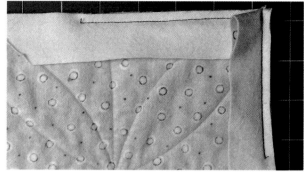

Sewing the second fold.

4. Sew the binding to the next side of the project.

5. Repeat steps 1 through 4 for the remaining sides of the project.

> ✱ **Laura's Hint**
>
> *As I sew the binding to the back side of the project, I trim small bits of fabric from the intersections that bow into the seam line.*

6. Trim the ends of the binding at a right-angle, leaving an overlap of ½".

7. Overlap the ends without turning back any seam allowance.

8. Stitch over the ends of the binding.

9. Fold the binding around the edge to the front side of the project.

10. On the front side of the project, topstitch in the center of the strip along the raw edge through all layers approximately ¼" from the fold. Note the finished edge is on the back of the project and the raw edge is on the front.

Straight-Grain Binding

Straight-grain binding may be used when there isn't sufficient fabric to cut long bias strips. By either hemstitching or serging along the front-facing edge, it can be made to look similar to the raw-edge binding.

1. Cut 1⅛" strips on the straight of grain.

2. Join as in steps 2 through 6 of the Miter instructions that came just before this section.

3. Using decorative thread, serge, hemstitch, or zigzag along one edge to stabilize the on-grain raw edge.

4. With right sides together, sew the unfinished edge of the binding strip to the back of the project, where it will be encased inside the folded binding.

5. Miter the corners as shown in the section just before this one.

6. Fold the serged edge to the front of the project and topstitch ¼" to ½" from the serged edge.

Finishing

Corner areas are prone to ravel because of the raw edges. This is easily avoided by pressing a scant drop of Fray Check™ deep into the corner joints of every intersection on both the front and back sides of the project.

Flowers

These blooming units are the focus of most projects. Star-shaped fabric cutouts are layered and folded. The bias-cut edges of the folded points are bent back and topstitched, forming the petals. These completed flower blocks are used individually or in multiples to comprise the basis for bags, purses, totes, and a variety of quilted projects.

Hexagon Flowers

Hexagon flowers are the simplest of the flower patterns. With just six petals, they are quick and easy to complete. Seven units will make a bathmat.

Templates

Prepare hexagon flower and fusible fleece templates as instructed on pages 118 and 119 (T-4 and T-5).

Cutting Plan

1. Cut 22" squares of fabric for each layer of the flower. If you need more than one flower unit, leave the fabric uncut.

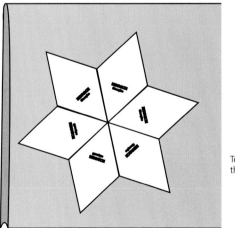

Template on the fabric.

2. Place the template on your fabric rotated so that no edge is parallel to the grain line. All edges will be cut on the bias to ease the petal turning and to minimize fraying.

3. With a rotary ruler on the outer lines of the template, cut the fabric star along the lines.

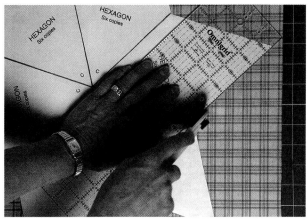

Cut with ruler and rotary cutter.

4. Cut the inner corners with a rotary point cutter or scissors.

5. Repeat steps 2 through 4 for the required number of pieces.

Fleece or Batting

Some projects will include a fleece or batting layer inside. Most flannel projects skip this step.

1. Cut fusible fleece or batting pieces using the T-5 template on page 119.

2. With the fusible web side down, center the fleece on the wrong side of the outer flower star.

3. With the right-side up and matching the outer edges, place the inner flower star on the fusible fleece and outer star.

4. Fold the points of both fabric stars to the center, as shown below, forming a hexagon. Press the folds.

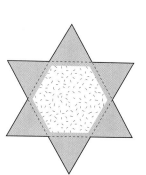

Place fleece in the center.

Match inner star on top.

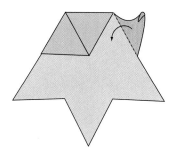

Fold the points in.

5. Topstitch ⅜" from the edge (over the folds) around all sides of the hexagon and sew a 2" circle of stitching at the center of the unit to tack down the points.

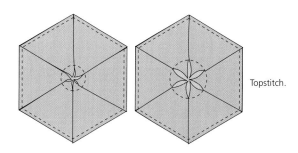

Topstitch.

6. To form petals, turn back the raw edges of the folded flaps between the center circle and outer topstitching.

7. Topstitch along all the raw edges, either with straight or decorative stitches.

8. At the center, fold back the petal points to reveal the inner fabric and stitch across the fold to the next petal.

✳ Laura's Hint

For a center stitching guide, cut a 2" circle of freezer paper, using the 2" circle template (T-12) on page 126, and press to the fabric.

Turn petals.

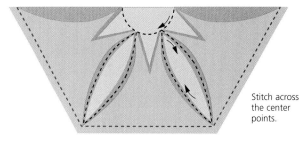

Stitch across the center points.

Octagon Flowers

These eight-petal flowers are so pretty and versatile. They're used in purses and totes, wall hangings, quilts, accessories, and as accents. There are four sizes, from extra small to large.

Templates

1. Prepare octagon flower and fusible fleece templates as instructed on pages 120 and 121 (T-6 and T-7).

2. For single flowers, cut two 21" squares of fabric: one for the inner layer and one for the outer layer.

3. Place the template on your fabric rotated so that no edge is parallel to the grain line. All edges will be cut on the bias to ease the petal turning and to minimize fraying.

4. With a rotary ruler on the outer lines of the template, cut the fabric star along the lines.

5. Cut the inner corners with a rotary point cutter or scissors.

Template on the fabric.

Cutting inner corners with point trimmer.

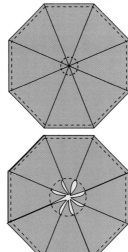

Cut the fabric with a ruler and rotary cutter.

6. Repeat entire process for the required number of pieces.

✳ Laura's Hint

Use the 2" circle template, page 126 (T-12) for the center stitching.

Fleece or Batting

Some projects will include a fleece or batting layer inside. Most flannel projects skip this procedure, however.

1. Cut fusible fleece or batting pieces using the template on page 121 (T-7).

2. With the fusible web side down, center the octagon-shaped piece of fleece on the wrong side of the outer flower star.

✳ Laura's Hint

I use a 10" circle of fleece, cut with either the template on page 126 or a 10" dinner plate.

Place the fleece.

3. With the right side out and matching the outer edges, place the inner flower star on the fusible fleece.

4. Fold the points of both fabric stars to the center, forming an octagon, as shown. Press the folds.

5. Topstitch ⅜" from the edge (over the folds) around all sides of the octagon and sew a 2" circle of stitching at the center of the unit to tack down the points.

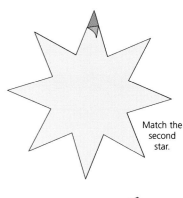

Match the second star.

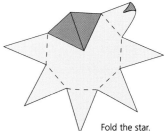

Fold the star.

Topstitch the unit.

7. Topstitch along all the raw edges, either with straight or decorative stitches.

8. At the center, open the petal points to reveal the inner fabric and stitch across each of the folds, as shown at right.

✳ Laura's Hints

✳ For a stitch guide, cut a circle of freezer paper and press it to the fabric.

✳ Varying the size of the circle will change the size of the petals formed in step 6.

6. Form flower petals by turning back the raw edges of the folded flaps between the center circle and outer topstitching.

Turn petals.

Sunflowers

These flowers burst with petals! Maximize your flower fun with sunnies.

Templates

Prepare the sunflower and fusible fleece templates as instructed on pages 124 and 125 (T-10 and T-11).

Cutting Plan

1. For single flowers, cut two 21" squares of fabric: one for the inner layer and one for the outer layer. For the red flower in the photo, for example, red is the inner layer and green is the outer layer.
2. Place the template on your fabric rotated so that no edge is parallel to the grain line. All edges will be cut on the bias to ease the petal-turning and to minimize fraying.
3. With a rotary ruler on the outer lines of the template, cut the fabric star along the lines.

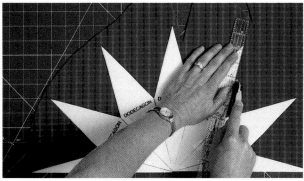

Template on the fabric.

Cutting with rotary cutter.

4. Cut the inner corners with a rotary point cutter or scissors.
5. Repeat the entire process for the required number of pieces.

❊ Laura's Hint

Use the 2" circle template, page 126 (T-12) for the center stitching.

Fleece or Batting

Some projects will include a fleece or batting layer inside. Most flannel projects, however, skip this procedure.

1. Cut fusible fleece or batting pieces using the template on page 125 (T-11).
2. With the fusible web side down, center a piece of fleece on the wrong side of the outer flower star.

❊ Laura's Hint

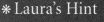

I use a 10" circle of fleece cut with either the template on page 126 or a 10" dinner plate.

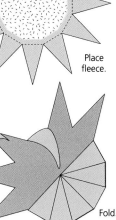

Place fleece.

Match the second star.

3. With the right side up and matching the outer edges, place the inner flower star on the fusible fleece and outer star.
4. Fold the points of both fabric stars to the center, forming a sunflower. Press the folds.
5. Topstitch ⅜" from the edge (over the folds) around all sides of the sunflower and sew a 2" circle of stitching at the center of the unit to tack down the points.
6. Form flower petals by turning back the raw edges of the folded flaps between the center and outer topstitching.
7. Topstitch along all the raw edges, either with straight or decorative stitches.

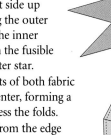

Fold.

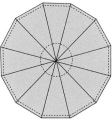

Topstitch.

❊ Laura's Hint

For a stitch guide, cut a circle of freezer paper and press it to the fabric.

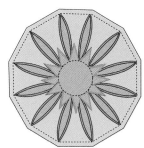

Turn back and topstitch the petals.

8. At the center, fold back the petal points to reveal the inner fabric and stitch across each of the folds.

Special Effect

For the daisy that is shown in the photo, insert a 2½" diameter circle of gold fabric in the center under the folded petals after step 7 above.

Leaves

Leaves form an attractive border for flowery quilts. They complete flower blocks in smaller projects. Create your own garden with leaf bases for your blooming bouquet.

Basic Leaves

Basic leaves are made from large, elongated triangle pieces that are folded to form a square or rectangle. Because you begin with rectangles, no template is needed. For larger blocks, the triangle is made from two pieces of fabric that are sewn together at the fold line.

Cutting Plan

1. With ruler and rotary cutter, cut fabric rectangles in the sizes specified in the project.
2. With right sides out, layer the two rectangles so the edges are even.
3. Find the center of the top by folding the two corners together and finger-press.
4. Using a ruler and rotary cutter, cut from the lower right corner to the top center point.
5. Cut from the lower left corner to the top center.

Finger-press the top center.

Cut from lower right to top center.

Cut the second side.

✳ Laura's Hint

Retain the leftover triangles. They can be used for the inner layer of additional projects.

Fleece or Batting

Most projects will include a fleece or batting layer inside for stiffness or loft. Flannel projects are heavy enough without an additional layer.

1. Cut a rectangle of fleece or batting in the size specified in the project.
2. With the lower edge centered on the triangle, place a rectangle of fleece (fusible side down) or batting between the fabric layers.
3. With the right side up, replace the top fabric triangle so that the edges are even.

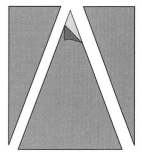

Center triangle.

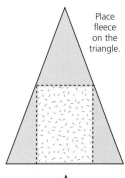

Place fleece on the triangle.

Replace top fabric.

4. Fold the three corners to the center of the bottom of the triangle.
5. Press the folds.

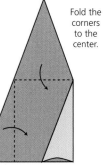

Fold the corners to the center.

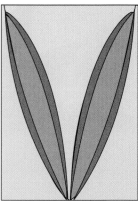

Press the folds.

6. Pin at the three points that meet at the center bottom.
7. Form the leaves by turning back the raw edges of the folded flaps between the pins and the upper outer-corner.
8. Stitch between the raw edge and the fold of the leaf.
9. Repeat steps 7 and 8 for the second leaf.

Turn back and topstitch the leaves.

10. Remove the pins.
11. With a slightly looser tension, add rows of quilting to "echo" the outline of the leaf pattern.

Three finished leaf units.

Outline quilting.

Mirror Leaves

Mirror leaf units are rectangles made from folded diamond-shaped pieces. (Again, because you begin with a rectangle, no template is needed.) Mirror leaves form the fronts and sides of some bags and the backs of others. Note that they are very similar to four-petal squares and the basic rectangle is the same.

Cutting Plan

1. With a ruler and rotary cutter, cut fabric rectangles in the sizes specified in the project.
2. With right sides out, layer the two rectangles so the edges are even.
3. Find the center of the top, bottom, and sides by folding the pieces in half and then in half again. Finger-press the center folds at the outside edges.
4. Using a ruler and rotary cutter, cut from the center bottom to the center right point.
5. Cut from the center right to the center top.
6. Cut from the top center to center left and then from center left to center bottom.

Find centers.

Cutting.

Cutting plan.

✳ Laura's Hint

Save the leftover triangles. They can be used for the inner layer of additional projects.

Fleece or Batting

Most projects will include a fleece or batting layer inside to create stiffness or loft. Flannel projects are heavy enough without an additional layer.

1. With ruler and rotary cutter, cut a rectangle of fleece or bating in the size specified in the project.

Place fleece.

2. Place a rectangle of fleece (fusible side down) or batting between the fabric layers so that it is centered on the diamond.
3. With right side up, replace the top fabric diamond so that the edges are even.

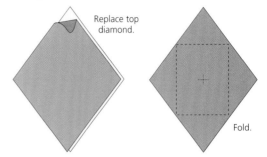

Replace top diamond.

Fold.

4. Fold the four corners to the center.
5. Press the folds and pin at the four corners.

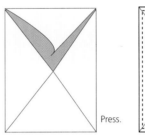 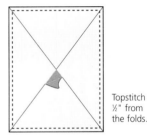

Press.

Topstitch ½" from the folds.

6. Topstitch ½" from the outer edge around all sides of the rectangle.
7. Form the leaves by turning back the raw edges of the folded flaps between the pins and the outer corner.
8. Stitch between the raw edge and the fold of the leaf.
9. Repeat steps 6 through 8 for the remaining leaves.

Turn back and topstitch the leaves.

Four mirror leaf units.

For another option, mix the two leaf styles.

Building Blocks

Three- and four-sided geometric shapes make great building blocks for flower projects. They are so versatile, serving as sides, ends, backs, bottoms—just about any supporting role. Sometimes they're flat, and sometimes they take on three-dimensional shapes to form a bag or tote.

Three-Petal Triangles

Triangles build pyramids. Stitch them together for a cute purse. Combine them with other shapes to make fun projects.

Templates

Prepare the triangle and fleece templates as instructed on pages 115 and 116 (T-1 and T-2).

Cutting Plan

1. Place the hexagon-shaped template on your fabric rotated so that no edge is parallel to the grain line. All edges will be cut on the bias.

2. With a rotary ruler on the outer lines of the template, use a rotary cutter to cut the fabric along the lines.

3. Cut fleece triangles with the template in the quantity specified in the pattern instructions.

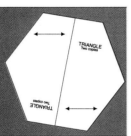

Template on fabric.

Cut with a ruler and rotary cutter.

✳ Laura's Hint

Fleece is used in most projects for its stiffness. Using fusible fleece keeps the pieces in place during construction. If fusible fleece is not available, use a light spray of temporary adhesive to keep the fleece or batting pieces in place. In some cases, batting will be specified when softness is desired.

4. With the fusible web side down, place a fleece triangle on the wrong side of an outer hexagon-shaped piece, as shown in the illustration.

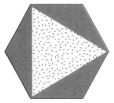

Place the fleece triangle.

5. With its right side out, layer the inner fabric hexagon over the fleece, matching it to the outer triangle.

6. Fold the three corners to the center and press the folds.

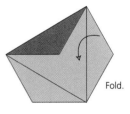

Fold.

7. Pin the corners at the center and topstitch ½" from the folds around the outer edge.

8. To form petals, turn back the bias cut edges of the folded flaps between the center pin and the outer top-stitching. Stitch along the curve, between the fold and the raw edge.

9. Stitch out to the top-stitching and back to the center for each of the three petals.

10. Repeat steps 4 through 9 for the number of triangles required for the project.

Place the top fabric.

Topstitching.

Turn back the petals.

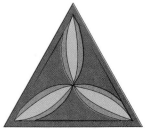

Complete unit.

Basic Squares with Four Petals

Squares have so many uses. They make up the building blocks in the Treasure Box and Four-Square Tote projects (pages 48 and 51, respectively). By themselves, they're cute as coasters.

Most projects call for square blocks in sizes that are cut using standard rotary rulers. A few are customized to better suit the project. Squares of fabric with bias-cut edges are folded into squares. The folds are turned to form petals and are then topstitched to complete the units. Use a rotary ruler or plastic template cut to the required size for these squares.

✳ Laura's Hint

Often, a standard-sized rotary ruler is the right size to cut the squares.

Cutting Plan

With a ruler and rotary cutter, cut squares with bias edges to ease petal turning and to minimize fraying. Use this cutting plan as a guide for 12½" bias squares.

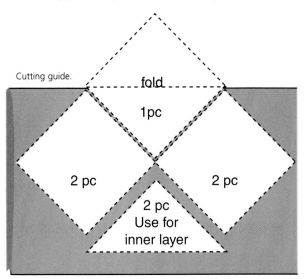

Cutting guide.

fold

1pc

2 pc

2 pc

2 pc
Use for
inner layer

Fleece or Batting

Lightweight fabrics, such as homespun, may need a light layer of batting. Purses need a stiffer fleece layer.

1. Cut fleece/batting squares to the size and quantity specified in the pattern instructions.
2. With the fusible side down, place a fleece square diagonally on the inside of the outer fabric square.
3. With the right side up, layer the inner square over the fleece, matching it to the outer square, as shown.

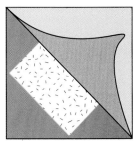

Place the fleece.

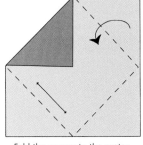

Grain line

Match the second square.

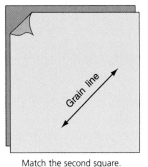

Fold the corners to the center.

4. Fold the four corners to the center and press the folds.

Optional Peek-a-Boo Version

If desired, place an on-grain square of an accent fabric after step 4 that is cut to fit inside the folded flaps.

5. Pin the corners at the center and topstitch ½" from the folds around the outer edge.

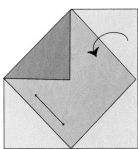

Place an accent square inside the folds.

Topstitch 1/2" from the fold.

6. To form petals, turn back the bias cut edges of the folded flaps between the center pin and the outer topstitching. Stitch along the curve, between the fold and the raw edge. Stitch out to the topstitching and back to the center for each of the four petals.
7. Repeat steps 2 through 6 for the number of squares required for the project.

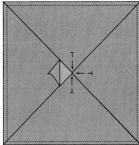

Turn back and topstitch the petals.

Basic Rectangles

Basic rectangles are the same as Basic and Mirror Leaves. Follow the instructions on page 23.

Modular Squares

Like an onion's skin, peel back the layers to reveal the inner fabrics.

Measurements are given for just one size and no template is needed. Note: the squares are cut on the straight of grain.

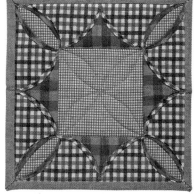

Cutting Plan

1. With ruler and rotary cutter, cut two 12½" squares. As illustrated, the blue square will be the back side and front outline of the finished block. The blue check square will be revealed when the top layers are folded back. It forms the center square and corner petal areas.

2. Cut two 10½" squares. These smaller squares will form the folds and curves on the front of the block.

✳ Laura's Hint

A 12½" square rotary ruler is just the right size to cut these squares.

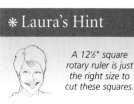

Cut two squares.

Fleece or Batting

1. Cut one 10½" square for each unit.

Assembly

1. Layer the green and dark blue 10½" squares with right sides out.

2. Cut the two 10½" squares diagonally.

3. Center the triangles on the outer edges of the right side of the larger square.

4. Lift one of the triangles and make a 1½"-long diagonal slash in the 12½" (blue check) square in the center of the area that will be covered by the folded triangle piece.

5. Make a template to mark the stitching guideline by cutting a 1¼" square of paper and folding it in half diagonally.

6. With the wrong side of the 12½" back side square (blue) facing up, place the paper triangle on each of the corners and mark along the folded edge. This is the seam guideline.

7. With right side down, place the back side 12½" square (blue) on top of the layered triangles.

8. Pin to secure all the layers.

9. Stitch a ¼" seam allowance around the sides. At the corners, stitch ¼" in from the diagonal guide line.

10. Trim the seam allowance to ⅛".

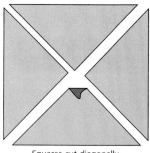

Squares cut diagonally.

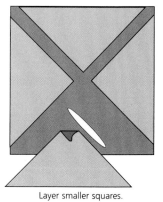

Layer smaller squares.

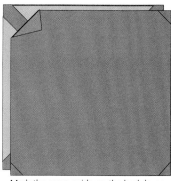

Mark the seam guide on the back layer.

Stitch and trim.

Fleece or Batting

If desired or required, add a layer of fleece.

1. Center a 10½"square of fleece on the uncut (back) side of the block.
2. Spray with temporary adhesive or fuse to secure in place.

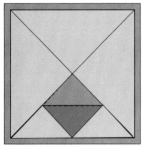

Place the fleece/batting.

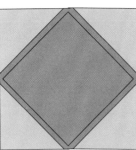

Turn right-side out.

3. Turn the block right side out through the slash and press.
4. Fold the corners to the center and press.

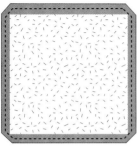

Fold the corners to the center.

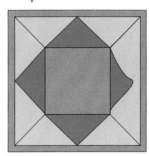

Fold the flaps.

5. Fold the flaps back onto themselves.
6. Pin and bend the bias edges to form petals.
7. Topstitch between the bias folds and the raw edges and quilt the center square.

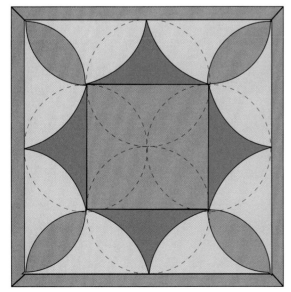

Turn and topstitch the petals.

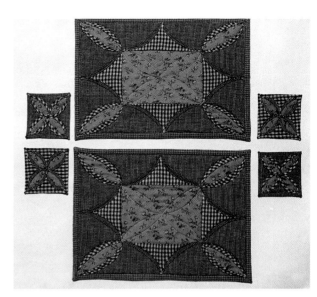

Modular Rectangles

These are an elongated version of the modular square and need no template. The rectangles provide an additional shape for interesting project variations. Measurements are given for just one size.

Cutting Plan

1. With a ruler and rotary cutter, cut two 13½" x 19½" rectangles. As illustrated, the dark pink rectangle will be the back side and front outline of the finished block. The light pink rectangle will be revealed when the top layers are folded back. It forms the center rectangle and corner petal areas.

Cut two rectangles.

2. Cut two 11¾" x 17¼" rectangles. These smaller rectangles will form the folds and curves on the front of the block.

Assembly

1. Layer the dark and light green smaller rectangles with right sides out.
2. Cut the two smaller rectangles diagonally.

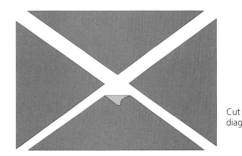

Cut diagonally.

3. Center the triangles on the outer edges of the right side of the larger rectangle.

4. Lift one of the triangles and make a 1½"-long diagonal slash in the larger (light pink) rectangle in the center of the area that will be covered by the folded triangle piece.

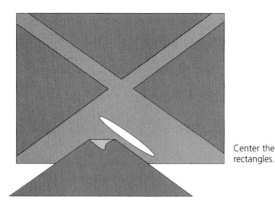

Center the rectangles.

5. Make a template to mark the stitching guideline by cutting a 1¼" rectangle of paper and folding it in half diagonally.

6. With the wrong side of the back side rectangle (dark pink) facing up, place the paper triangle on each of the corners and draw a line along the folded edge. This is the seam guideline.

7. With right side down, place this rectangle (dark pink) on top of the layered triangles and pin to secure all the layers.

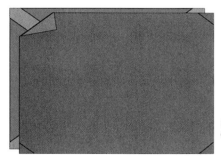

Place back on top.

8. Stitch a ¼" seam allowance around the sides. At the corners, stitch ¼" in from the diagonal guideline. Trim the seam allowance to ⅛".

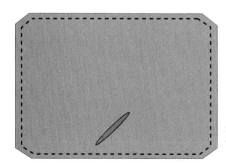

Stitch and trim.

Fleece or Batting

If desired or required, add a layer of fleece.
1. Cut one 12" x 17" rectangle for each unit.

2. Center a rectangle of fleece on the uncut (back) side of the block.

3. Spray with temporary adhesive or fuse to secure in place.

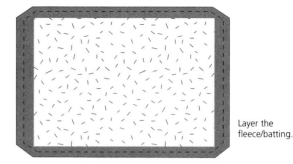

Layer the fleece/batting.

4. Turn the block right-side out through the slash and press.

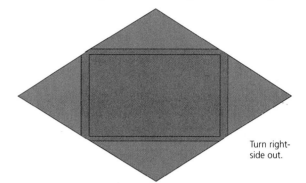

Turn right-side out.

5. Fold the corners to the center and press.

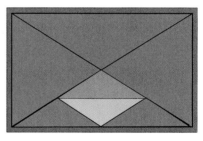

Fold the corners to the center.

6. Fold the flaps back onto themselves and pin.

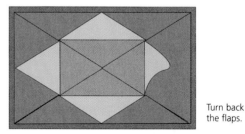

Turn back the flaps.

7. Bend the bias edges to form petals, top-stitch between the bias folds and the raw edges, and quilt the center rectangle.

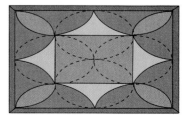

Form the petals.

Diamonds

This simple shape makes wonderful optical illusions. It also nicely fills in hexagon corners.

Templates

1. Prepare the diamond and fleece templates as instructed on pages 117 and 118 (T-3 and T-4).
2. Place the diamond template on the fabric noting the grain line marking, as shown in the illustration.

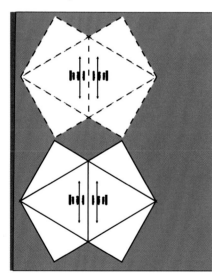

Place the template on the fabric.

Cutting Plan

1. With a ruler and rotary cutter, cut the fabric along the solid outer lines of the template.

Cut with a ruler and rotary cutter.

2. Cut the inner corners with a rotary point tool or scissors.
3. Cut the number of fleece inserts specified in the project instructions.

Assembly

1. Center a fleece insert on the wrong side of the outer fabric piece.

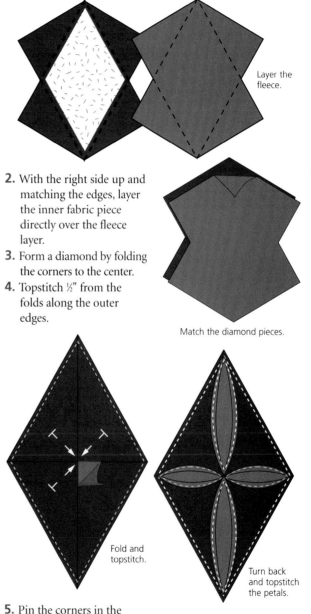

Layer the fleece.

2. With the right side up and matching the edges, layer the inner fabric piece directly over the fleece layer.
3. Form a diamond by folding the corners to the center.
4. Topstitch ½" from the folds along the outer edges.

Match the diamond pieces.

Fold and topstitch.

Turn back and topstitch the petals.

5. Pin the corners in the middle.
6. Form petals by turning back the bias-cut edges of the folded flaps between the center pins and the outer topstitching. Stitch along the curves between the fold and the raw edge.

Patches and Parts

Patches are used to fill the spaces left between flower blocks. Squares fill in octagon flowers, diamonds fill in hexagons, and triangles fill in sunflowers.

They are constructed like little pillows, with a layer of fleece between two sheets. The layers are stitched together to prevent shifting. To minimize shredding, the fabric is cut so that raw edges are on the bias.

To "install" the patches, they are placed either on the front or back side of the opening and stitched around the margins. Choosing patches in contrasting colors can create unique patterns.

Parts to complete your project include handles and some structural elements (backs, bottoms, and sides). Simple folded fabric with a fleece core is used to make handles for totes and bags. Plain backs, bottoms, and sides were designed to simplify project design. They form the structure of several bags and totes. The simple layering of fabric and fleece are quick to complete.

Squares, Half-Squares, and Quarter-Squares Patches

Note that square and half-square patches can also be made from "four-leaf" blocks, page 23.

Cutting Plan

1. With a ruler and rotary cutter, cut 5" squares on the bias using a ruler and a rotary cutter. In most octagon flower projects, you will need to cut whole, half-, and quarter-squares. Begin by cutting whole squares, noting that you will need some for the top and some for the back side of your project.
2. Half-squares are made by folding whole squares diagonally in half. Similarly, quarters are made from half-square triangles folded diagonally.

Fleece or Batting

1. Cut 4" strips of fleece.
2. Crosscut the strips into 4" squares.
3. Cut the squares diagonally into halves and cut diagonally again for quarters.

Cut batting diagonally.

Square Assembly

1. With right sides out, center the 4" square of batting or fleece between two 5" bias-cut fabric squares and pin.
2. Stitch through all the layers.

Layer the fleece between the fabric squares.

✳ Laura's Hint

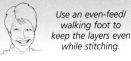

Use an even-feed/walking foot to keep the layers even while stitching.

3. Stitch diagonally to secure the center area.

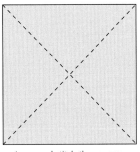

Layer and stitch the squares.

Half-Square Assembly

1. With right side out, fold a 5" square in half diagonally and press.
2. Center a half-square of fleece/batting between the layers.

3. Stitch through all the layers. See the photo for suggested stitching lines. (See hint for keeping the layers even while stitching.)

Fold and stitch the half-squares.

Quarter-Square Assembly

1. Cut a 5" bias-square in half diagonally.
2. With the right side out, fold in half and press.
3. Center a quarter-square of fleece between the layers.
4. Stitch through all the layers, referring to the photo for suggested stitching lines. (See hint for keeping the layers even while stitching.)

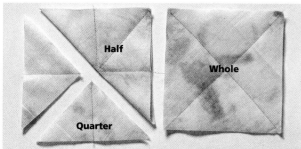

Half

Whole

Quarter

Stitch the quarter-squares.

Installing Square Patches

1. Position the patch over the area in your piece that needs to be patched and pin.
2. With sewing machine, hemstitch the patch in place.

Hemstitch the patch.

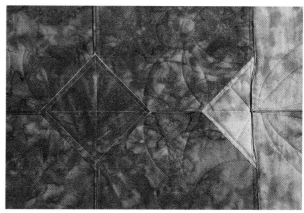

Inserted square patches on the back side.

Triangle Patches

Use these in sunflower projects to fill in the center and edge areas.

Templates

Prepare triangle patch and batting templates as instructed on page 125 (T-11).

Cutting Plan

1. Place the template on the fabric with the proper alignment to the grain line.
2. Cut the fabric triangles using the template, ruler, and rotary cutter.

✱ Laura's Hint

The pieces left from cutting the sunflowers have two perfect corners for triangles. Place the template on the corner and cut the third side.

Cut triangles from leftovers.

Fleece or Batting

1. Cut a 2¼" strip of fleece.
2. Using the template, cut the triangles from the strip.

3. Center the batting between the top and bottom layer of triangles and pin.

4. Stitch through all the layers.

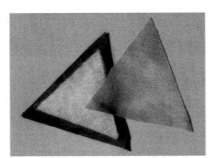
Layer the triangles.

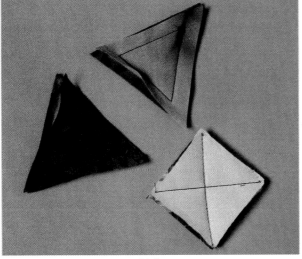
Stitch.

Installing Triangle Patches

1. Find the gap between sunflowers and position the patch over the area in your piece that needs to be patched, either on the front or back side of the project. Pin.

* Laura's Hint

To minimize shifting of the layers, stitch around using an even-feed/ walking foot on your sewing machine.

Note the gap between the sunflowers.

Triangle patch on the front.

Triangle patch on the back.

2. Place fusible web strips on the edges of the triangle and press to fuse the triangle in place.

3. Stitch along the raw edges of the patch through all layers with either a hemstitch or zigzag stitch.

Place the fusible web strips.

Patching the Outer Edges

1. Fill in the area along the outer edge of the joined
sunflowers with triangle patches.

Place triangle near the edge.

Pin triangle in place.

2. Overlap the raw edges of the triangle, even with the outer
edges of the sunflower units and pin.

3. Stitch along the raw edges of the patch through all layers
with either a hemstitch or zigzag stitch.

Here are examples of same-color or contrasting
color triangle patches: same-color patches (left)
and contrasting patches.

Diamond Patches

Diamond patches are made the same way as diamond blocks. Instructions are detailed on page 29.

For some projects, the diamonds are cut in half lengthwise, as shown.

Cut diamond patch in half.

Handles

Handles are made from fabric strips wrapped around a fleece core. Lighter weight handles have fewer layers of fabric or are made without the fleece core. They are more flexible and soft and are usually used for smaller bags and totes.

Assembly

1. Cut the fabric and fleece strips as specified in the project instructions.

2. Fold the fabric in half lengthwise and press.

Fold the rectangle in half lengthwise.

3. Place the fleece strip in between the folded fabric.

Insert the fleece strip.

4. Wrap one raw edge of the fabric around the fleece strip and press.

Fold raw edge over the fleece.

5. Turn the remaining raw edge under and press.

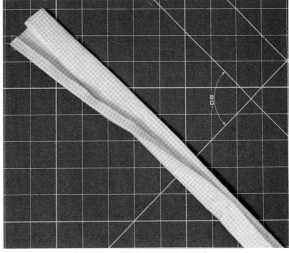

Turn the remaining raw edge under.

6. Match the two folded edges, refolding so all raw edges are encased, as shown below. Press.

Fold the piece a third time.

7. Topstitch ¼" from the folds along both sides and in the middle, as shown below.

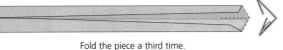

Topstitch.

Attaching Outside Handles

1. With right sides together, place the raw end of the handle ¼" above the stitching line and pin.
2. Stitch ¼" from the raw edge.
3. Repeat steps 1 and 2 for the remaining end.
4. Fold the handle up over the seam and pin.
5. Stitch ¼" from the fold. Back-tack to secure the seam.

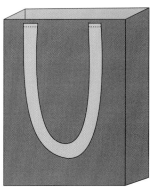

With the raw edge up, pin handles inside and stitch.

Attaching Inside Handles

For some tote bags, handles are placed inside the bag.

1. With the right side of the handle on the inside of the bag, place a raw end of the handle ¼" above the stitching line and pin.
2. Stitch ¼" from the raw edge.
3. Fold the handle up over the seam and pin.
4. Stitch ¼" from the fold. Back-tack to secure the seam.

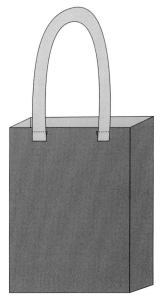

Fold handles up and stitch.

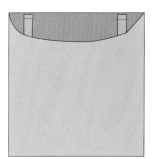

With the raw edge up, pin handles inside and stitch.

Fold handles up and topstitch.

Bottoms, Sides, and Backs

These rectangular or square pieces complete the bottoms and backs of totes and purses. They are constructed of inner and outer fabric layers fused around a layer of fleece. Edges are finished with zigzag stitching to prevent raveling.

Bottom

1. With ruler and rotary cutter, cut the fabric and fleece rectangles as specified in the project.

Cut the fabric and fleece rectangles.

2. With right sides out, center the fleece between the fabric pieces and press to fuse the fleece.

Layer the fleece.

3. On the non-fused side, insert a rectangle of fusible web and press to fuse.

Insert fusible web.

4. Zigzag stitch over the raw edges.

Zigzag.

Side

1. Prepare side piece as in steps 1 through 4 of the bottom instructions.

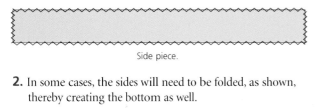

Side piece.

2. In some cases, the sides will need to be folded, as shown, thereby creating the bottom as well.

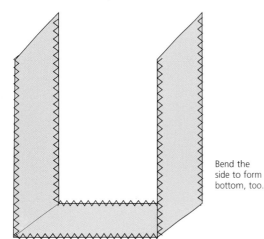

Bend the side to form bottom, too.

Back

For some projects, the back is made the same as a bottom, with all four sides having raw edges. When it's desirable to have a finished edge, use this method with the folded back piece.

1. With the right side out, fold the back fabric piece crosswise in half. Press.

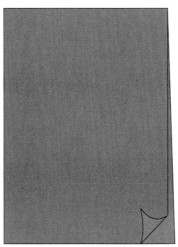

Fold the fabric for the back piece.

2. Place the fleece centered between the folded fabric and press to fuse.

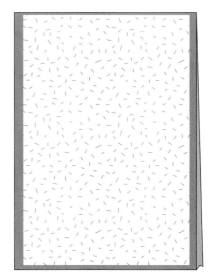

Layer fleece.

3. On the non-fused side, insert the fusible web and press to fuse.

4. Zigzag over the three unfinished sides.

5. Orient the folded side of the back piece to the top of your project.

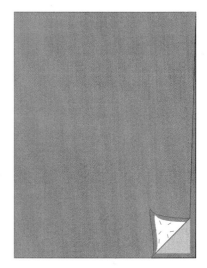

Insert fusible web.

Zigzag over the raw edges.

# 2 Blooming Flower Accessories and Bags

On vacation, I saw a collection of quilted purses. Inspiration! Since the flower units are geometric, it was a short leap to building them into three-dimensional shapes. Like topsy, they grew and grew. Anything that will fit together has been made into an accessory, tote, or purse.

Eyeglass/Coin/Neck Pouches

These soft cases work great for carrying reading glasses or small change and are great to travel with. They are just the right size and are easy to make. Pop one into your purse. Directions are given for the eyeglass case. The modifications for other sizes are shown in the chart at the end of the project instructions.

Triangle eyeglass pouch variation.

Finished Size

3½" x 6½"

Fabric and Notions

* ¼-yard gold plaid
* ¼-yard gold check
* ⅛-yard fusible fleece
* ⅛-yard fusible web
* 1" strip hook-and-loop tape

Template

Small triangle template, page 116 (T-2, cut on the red line)

Cutting Plan

From the gold plaid, cut:
* 4" x 16" rectangle (outside)
* 5" square (outside triangle)

From the gold check, cut:
* 4" x 16" rectangle (inside)
* 5" square (inside triangle)

From the fleece, cut:
* 3½" x 12" rectangle

From the fusible web, cut:
* 3½" x 12" rectangle

Assembly

Make one small triangle.

1. Using the two 5" squares and the T-2 template, prepare one small triangle, as instructed on page 24. Set the finished triangle aside.

2. With right sides together, stitch across one short end of the two 4" x 16" rectangles.

Layer the rectangle pieces.

3. With the adhesive side down, place the fleece rectangle at the stitching line and fuse it in place.

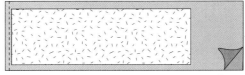

Layer the fleece.

4. Turn the strips right-side out.

Turn right-side out.

5. Place the 3½" x 12" rectangle of fusible web over the fleece and fuse it in place.

6. To form the pocket area, fold the fleece-lined section in half, so the fleece ends are even.

(continued)

7. Fold the top, unlined section with the finished edge overlapping the first folded piece by ½", as shown at right.

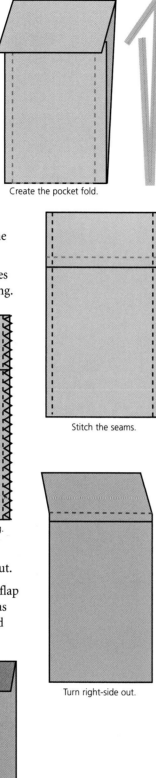

Create the pocket fold.

8. Stitch ¼" seam allowance along the two raw edges.

9. Finish the raw edges with zigzag stitching.

Stitch the seams.

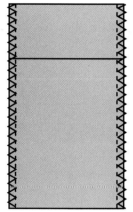

Finish with zigzag stitching.

10. Turn right-side out.

11. Fold the unlined flap over the pocket, as shown below, and press.

Turn right-side out.

Fold the flap.

12. Overlap one side of the triangle piece so it is centered on the flap, pin, and topstitch ⅛" in from the edge of the triangle, as shown at right.

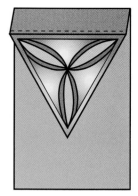

Topstitch the triangle to the flap.

Coin purse variation.

Size Variation Chart

Style	Finished Size	Rectangles	Fold at:	Template	Fleece
Coin	4" square	4½" x 10"	3½"	T-9 XS	3¾" x 7"
Neck Pouch*	4" x 5½"	4½" x 14"	5½"	T-9 XS	3¾" x 11"
Large Eyeglass	4" x 6"	4½" x 15"	6"	T-9 XS	3¾" x 12"
Triangle Eyeglass	3½" x 6"	4" x 15"	6"	T-2 SM	3" x 12"

*1 yard of cotton cord also needed.

Large eyeglass pouch variation.

A different look is created by using batik for the flower.

Neck pouch variation.

Zippy Coin Purse

Here's a handy little accessory. The construction is simply the joining of two small octagon flowers with a zipper across the top. There are two sizes for versatility.

Finished Size

Extra Small, 4½"
(Small, 5½")

Fabric and Notions

✳ ¼-yard or a fat quarter blue
✳ ¼-yard or a fat quarter yellow
✳ 4" (7") zipper

Template

Extra small (small) octagon template, page 123 (T-9)

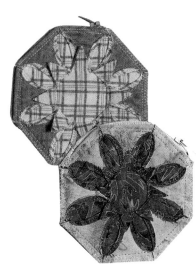

Combine different colors to create cute variations.

Batik coin purse option.

Cutting Plan

From the blue, cut:
✳ two 8½" squares (octagon flower outside layers)

From the yellow, cut:
✳ two 8½" squares (octagon flower inside layers)

Assembly

1. Prepare two octagon flower units, either extra small or small, as instructed on pages 19-20.

Make two octagon flower units.

2. With the two octagon flowers right-side up, pin the zipper to the flower pieces, and stitch it in place, as shown below.

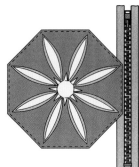

Stitch zipper across the top.

3. With right sides out, match the corners of the flower units and pin.

4. Zigzag over the edge from one end of the zipper to the other, as shown at right, back-tacking at the beginning and the end of the stitching.

Zigzag stitch between the ends of the zipper.

Calendar/Checkbook Cover

D ress up your calendar or checkbook with this simple cover. Two rectangle blocks form the outside. The inside has two flaps to insert the cover. Give these as gifts to your organized friends.

Finished Size

4" x 7"

Fabric and Notions

* ⅓-yard dark print
* ¼-yard light print
* ⅛-yard fusible web
* 1 yard single-fold bias tape

Template

None needed.

Front view of calendar cover.

Cutting Plan

From the dark print, cut:
* two 8" x 14" rectangles (outer mirror leaf units)
* two 6" x 7" rectangles (inner pockets)

From the light print, cut:
* two 8" x 14" rectangles (inner mirror leaf units)

From the fusible web, cut:
* two 3" x 7" rectangles

Assembly

1. Prepare two mirror leaf units, as instructed on page 23.
2. With right sides up, butt the two longer sides together.
3. Zigzag across the seam, as shown below.

Join the rectangles with zigzag stitching.

4. Fold the two 6" x 7" rectangles of fabric in half to measure 3" x 7".
5. Layer the fusible web evenly between the folds and press to fuse.
6. Place the folded rectangles on the inside of the outer edges of the mirror leaf blocks and pin in place.

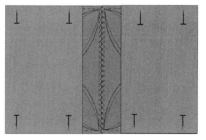

Place the inner rectangles.

7. Wrap the outside, including the inner rectangles, with the bias tape. Pin and stitch ¼" from the edge.

Add the binding.

Name Tag or Place Card

Transform your fabric scraps into these handy name tags or place markers. They're great for guild meetings or social events.

Finished Size

4" x 4" x ¼"

Fabric and Notions

* 5" square green
* 8½" square yellow
* 8½" square plaid
* 3" square embroidery stabilizer
* 1 safety pin

Template

Extra small octagon flower template, page 123 (T-9)

✳ Laura's Hint

If desired, use a 5" square scrap of fabric to practice embroidering the name before completing the real one in step 5.

Finished name tag.

Cutting Plan

From the green, cut:
* one 5" square (name inlay)

From the yellow, cut:
* one extra small octagon flower (inside flower layer)

From the plaid, cut:
* one extra small octagon flower (outside flower layer)

Assembly

1. Prepare one extra small octagon flower, as instructed on pages 19-20, stopping at Fleece or Batting step 6, so the petals will remain unstitched.
2. Find the center of the green square by folding it in half and then in half again.
3. Pinch to finger-press the folds.
4. Place embroidery stabilizer on the back side of the green square with a spritz of temporary adhesive spray.
5. Stitch the first name above the horizontal fold line and the last name just below the fold, with the letters centered at the vertical fold.

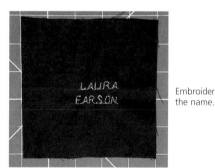

Embroider the name.

6. Prepare the name tag template on page 123.
7. Place it over the stitched name so that the name is centered in the "window" of the template, as shown at right.

Center the template over the name.

8. Using the template, ruler, and rotary cutter, trim the extra fabric.

Cut with the ruler, template, and rotary cutter.

9. Open the flower unit and insert the green name layer. Refold so all layers are flat.

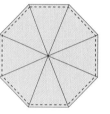

Insert the name layer inside the flower.

10. Topstitch ¼" from the outer folds.

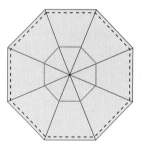

Topstitch ¼" from the folds.

11. With the template and a fabric marker, draw the smaller octagon onto the folded points, as shown. This is the center stitching line.

Mark the center stitching line with the template.

12. Pin the points to the center.
13. Complete the octagon flower, as instructed in steps 7 and 8 on page 20.
14. If using as a name tag, sew a safety pin to center of the back side.

Treasure Box

Fill this with your special treats and present it as a gift. Or, use it on your dresser as a holder for cotton balls, makeup sticks, or tissues. It's made from six basic squares stitched together. The lid is fastened with a loop.

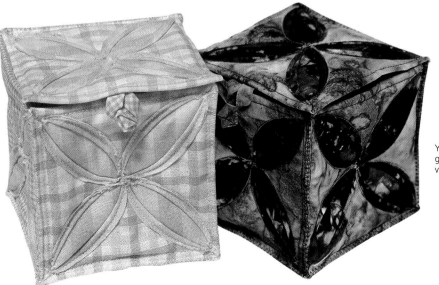

Yellow and green box variations.

Finished Size

4" cube

Fabric and Notions

* ½-yard light green
* ½-yard dark green

Template

None needed.

Cutting Plan

From the light green, cut:
* six 6" bias-cut squares (outside)

From the dark green, cut:
* six 6" bias-cut squares (inside)

Assembly

1. Prepare six basic squares, as instructed on page 25.

Create six basic squares with four petals.

2. With right sides out, layer two squares and zigzag stitch over the edges to join them together.

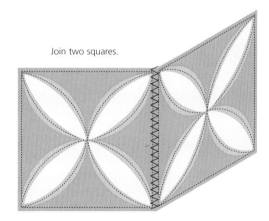

Join two squares.

3. Open the joined pair, place a third square right-side up on one of the paired squares, and pin as needed.

4. Zigzag stitch where the units are being joined, as shown.

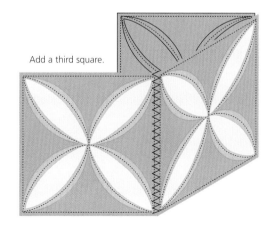

Add a third square.

(continued)

5. Match the corners of the fourth square to the corners of the joined squares to form the bottom of the box, pin, and zigzag over the edges of the matched squares.

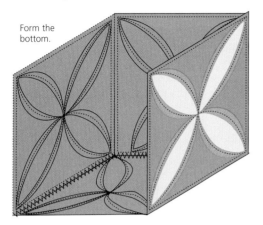

Form the bottom.

6. Match the corners of the fifth square, with its right side out, to those of the joined squares to complete the body of the box.

Finish the box.

7. With its right side up, match the sixth square to one of the open sides of the box to form the lid, pin, and zigzag at the joint.

Add the top.

For the closure:

1. Fold a 2" binding strip into a loop, as shown.

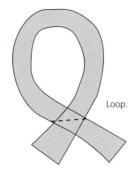

Loop.

2. Pin to the center front, inside the box lid.

3. Stitch across the fold.

4. Knot a 3" strip of binding, leaving a 1" tail. Tuck one raw end of the strip into the knot.

5. Stitch across the knot.

6. Put the knot through the loop.

7. Pin the remaining raw end of the knot to the center inside of the front square.

8. Stitch across the tail through the square.

Four-Square Tote

Carry your books to class or pick up some groceries with this handy tote. It's quick to make four basic squares for the front. The back is a layer of fleece sandwiched between two fabric squares. It's completed with simple handles. Two sizes are given.

Finished Size

Medium, 11" square
[Small, 8" square]*

*Measurements for the small size will be in brackets.

Fabric and Notions

* ⅓-yard [⅓-yard] orange
* ⅓-yard [⅓-yard] multicolor check
* ⅔-yard [½-yard] blue
* 12" [8"] square fusible fleece
* 12" [8"] square fusible web
* 1" strip hook-and-loop tape

Template

None needed.

Finished tote.

Cutting Plan

From the orange, cut:
* two 8½" [6"] bias-cut squares (front)

From the blue, cut:
* four 8½" [6"] bias-cut squares (front)
* one 12" x 24" [8" x 16"] rectangle (back)
* one 3"-wide selvedge-to-selvedge strip cut in half (handles)

From the multicolor check, cut:
* two 8½" [6"] bias-cut squares (front)

From the fusible fleece, cut:
* one 12" [8"] square
* two 1" x 20" [one 1" x 16"] strips (handles)

From the fusible web, cut:
* one 12" [8"] square

Assembly

1. Mixing the colors for the inner and outer layers, prepare four basic squares, as instructed on page 25.
2. With right sides up, butt two of the squares along the folded edges.
3. Join squares together with zigzag stitching.
4. Repeat steps 2 and 3 above for the remaining two squares.

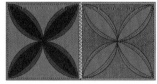

Join two squares with zigzag stitching.

5. Open the seams and finger-press.

Complete the second two squares.

6. With the corners and centers matched, pin, and join the two pairs with a zigzag stitch.

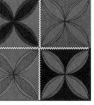

Join two pairs.

For the back:

1. Prepare the back piece, as instructed on page 36.
2. With the folded edge of the back toward the top and with right sides together, place the four-flower piece on top of the back piece and pin.

Position the back piece.

3. Stitch a ¼" seam allowance along the three raw edges, back-tacking at the corners.

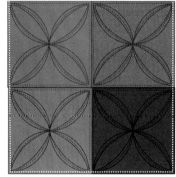

Stitch back.

4. Turn right sides out.

For the handles:

1. Prepare the handles, as instructed on pages 34-35.
2. Position handles inside the top edge of the front and back of the bag, pin, and stitch in place.

Horizontal Book Tote

This book tote, and the vertical variation that follows it, are so handy for kids. Have one for the library and one for school. Make several to have on hand for gifts. Leftovers from this project can be used for the vertical tote leaf units and vice versa.

Finished Size

10" x 7½" x 1"

Fabric and Notions

* ⅔-yard dark green
* ½-yard light green
* ⅓-yard yellow
* ⅓-yard fusible fleece
* 8" x 10" fusible web
* 1" strip hook-and-loop tape

Template

Small octagon flower template, page 123 (T-9)

Cutting Plan

From the dark green, as illustrated, cut:
* one 16" x 20" rectangle cut diagonally (A sections for leaves)
* one 8½" square (flower)
* one 10" x 16" rectangle folded to 8" x 10" (back side)
* two 2" x 26" strips (sides)
* one 1" x 22" strip (binding)

From the light green, as illustrated, cut:
* one 16" x 20" rectangle cut diagonally (A sections for leaves)

From the yellow, cut:
* one 8½" square (flower)

From the fusible fleece, cut:
* two 3½" x 9½" rectangles (leaves)
* one 7½" x 9½" rectangle (back)
* two 1" x 17" strips (handles)
* one 1¾" x 26" strip (sides)

From the fusible web, cut:
* one 8" x 10" rectangle (back)
* one 1" x 26" strip (sides)

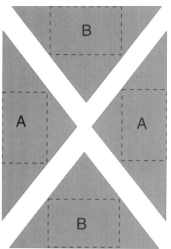

Cutting plan for leaves.

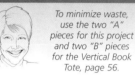

✳ Laura's Hint

To minimize waste, use the two "A" pieces for this project and two "B" pieces for the Vertical Book Tote, page 56.

Assembly

1. Prepare two 4" x 10" basic leaf units, as instructed on page 22.

2. Using the 8½" squares of dark green and yellow fabric, prepare a small octagon flower unit, as instructed on pages 19-20.

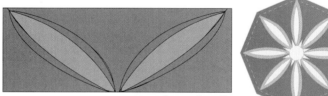

Prepare the units.

3. Join the two leaf units with zigzag stitching across the seam, as shown at right.

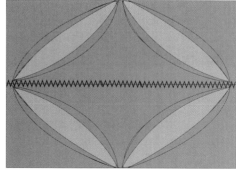

Join the leaf units.

4. Center the flower between the leaf units and topstitch in place, as shown below.

Attach the flower to the front.

For the back and side:

1. Prepare the back and side/bottom pieces, as instructed on page 36.

2. With right sides together, match the center of the side/bottom piece to the center of the front piece and pin at the center and at the corners, as shown below.

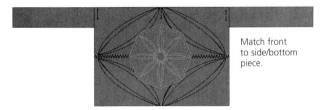

Match front to side/bottom piece.

3. Stitch ¼" seam allowance on three sides.

4. With right sides together and the fold at the top, match the back piece to the side piece and pin.

5. Stitch ¼" seam allowance on the three matched sides, as shown below.

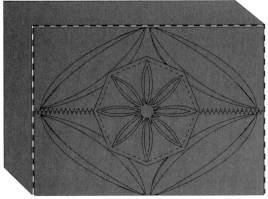

Stitch the bottom/side piece.

6. Turn right-side out.

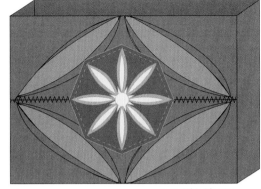

Turn right-side out.

For the binding:

1. Fold the 1" x 22" strip in half lengthwise and press.

2. Open the strip, fold the raw edges lengthwise into the first fold, and press.

3. Starting at a side seam, wrap the folded binding tape over the top edge of the tote. Rip a few stitches in the side seam and insert the raw ends into the seam.

4. Stitch along the edge of the binding and re-stitch the side seam.

5. Prepare the two handles, as instructed on pages 34-35.

6. Position the handles to the inside of the front and back sides of the tote, pin, and stitch in place.

7. Apply the hook-and-look tape to the inside of the top center of the bag.

Finished tote.

Vertical Book Tote

L ike its cousin, the Horizontal Book Tote (pages 53-55), this little bag can serve as a carrier for books or a knitting project. The cutting plan is set up so that you'll get both from the allotted fabric.

Finished Size

7" x 10" x 2½"

Fabric and Notions

* 1 yard dark green
* ½-yard light green
* ⅓-yard yellow
* ⅓-yard fusible fleece
* 8" x 10" rectangle fusible web
* 2½" x 28" rectangle fusible web
* 1" strip hook-and-loop tape

Template

Medium octagon flower template, page 122 (T-8)

Cutting Plan

From the dark green, as illustrated, cut:
* one 16" x 20" rectangle
   cut diagonally (B sections for leaves)
* one 12" square (flower)
* one 8½" x 10½" rectangle (front blank)
* one 8" x 20" rectangle
   folded to 8" x 10" (back)
* two 2" x 26" strips (sides/bottom)

From the light green, cut:
* one 16" x 20" rectangle (B sections for leaves)

From the yellow, cut:
* one 12" square (flower)

From the fusible fleece, cut:
* one 5" x 7" rectangle (leaf)
* one 7" x 9½" rectangle (back)
* two 1" x 17" strips (handles)
* one 1¼" x 26"strip (sides)

From the fusible web, cut:
* one 8" x 10" rectangle (back)
* one 2½" x 28"strip (sides/bottom)

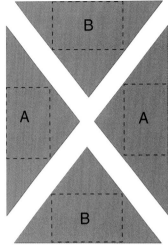

Cutting plan for leaves.

✳ Laura's Hint

To minimize waste, use the two "B" pieces for this project and two "A" pieces for the Horizontal Book Tote, page 53.

Assembly

1. Prepare the two 5" x 8" basic leaf units, as instructed on page 22, and the small octagon flower, as detailed on pages 19-20.

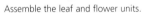

Assemble the leaf and flower units.

2. Fold the 8½" x 10½" front blank rectangle in half to measure 5¼" x 8½".

3. Prepare the blank and the back, as instructed on page 36.

4. Prepare the side section, as instructed on page 36.

(continued)

5. With the fold toward the top, join the front blank to one basic leaf block with zigzag stitching.

6. Center the small octagon flower on the front and pin in place, as shown below.

Pin the flower to the front.

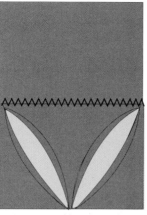

Join blank and leaf units.

7. Topstitch around the edge of the flower through all layers.

8. With right sides together, match the bottom center of the front piece to the center of the side/bottom section and pin in the center and at the corners.

Pin the front to the side piece.

9. Stitch ¼" seam allowance around the three sides, back-tacking at the beginning and the end.

10. With right sides together and the fold toward the top, match the bottom center of the back piece to the center of the side/bottom section and pin in the center and at the corners.

11. Stitch ¼" seam allowance around the three sides. Back stitch at the beginning and at the end.

Stitch the bottom/side piece to the front.

12. Turn right-side out.

13. Prepare the two handles, as instructed on pages 34-35.

14. Position the handles to the inside of the front and back sides of the tote, pin, and stitch in place.

Turn right-side out.

Finished tote.

Magic Square Tote

I t's perfect for a day of shopping or carrying your knitting. Stitch this in no time. Fold back the petals on this bag to reveal the many layers of fabric that form soft curves.

Finished Size

10½" x 10½" x 3¾"

Fabric and Notions

* ⅜-yard chambray
* ⅜-yard blue gingham
* ⅜-yard small plaid
* ⅜-yard large plaid
* ⅜-yard fusible fleece.
* 1" strip hook-and-loop tape

Template

None needed. A 12½" square rotary ruler is just the right size to cut the squares.

❋ Laura's Hint

To find the centers in step 5, fold the piece in half and pin at the fold.

Finished bag.

Cutting Plan

From the chambray, cut:
* two 12½" squares (outer edge and inside)
* two 4" x 7" rectangles (bottom)
* two 3" x 12" strips (handles)

From the blue gingham, cut:
* two 12½" squares (inner reveal area)

From the small plaid, cut:
* two 10½" squares (folded petals)

From the large plaid, cut:
* two 10½" squares (folded petals)

From the fusible fleece, cut:
* two 10½" squares (front and back)
* one 3½" x 6½" rectangle (bottom)
* two ¾" x 12" strips (handles)

Assembly

1. Prepare two modular squares, as instructed on page 26.

2. Prepare the bottom, as instructed on page 35-36.

3. With the right sides together, join the two modular squares along one side with a ⅛" seam allowance, as shown at right. Back-tack at the beginning and the end.

4. Unfold the joined squares and press the seam flat.

5. Find the center of one square and the center of one long side of the bottom piece, match the centers of the two pieces as shown at right, and pin.

6. Pin the corners of the bottom piece to the square and continue pinning along the bottom piece.

7. Stitch a ¼" seam allowance along the pinned edges, as shown.

8. With the partially assembled bag inside-out, join the remaining side of the bag with a ⅛" seam, as shown at right.

9. Prepare the handles, as instructed on pages 34-35.

10. Attach the handles to the inside of the top edge, as shown on page 35.

11. Apply the hook-and-loop tape to the inside top center.

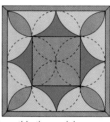

Assemble the modular squares.

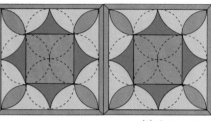

Join two squares.

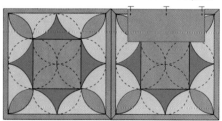

Match the bottom to the squares.

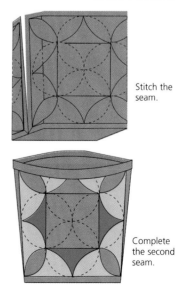

Stitch the seam.

Complete the second seam.

Tiny Tote Bag

Perfect for the girl in your life. This tiny tote has two pockets to hold the necessities–keys, cards, or lipstick. Make several for holiday gift-giving.

Finished Size

4½" x 9" x 3";
15" to the top of the handle

Fabric and Notions

* 1 fat quarter large-flower print
* ½-yard gold print
* 1 fat quarter navy dotted print
* 1 fat quarter navy print
* 1 fat quarter solid navy
* ¼-yard fusible fleece
* ¼-yard fusible web
* 1" strip hook-and-loop tape

Templates

* Small octagon flower template, page 123 (T-9)
* 5" circle, page 126 (T-12)

Finished bag.

Cutting Plan

From the large-flower print, cut:
* two 3½" x 17½" rectangles (handle)

From the gold print, cut:
* two 3½" x 17½" rectangles (handle lining)
* two 10" squares (inner flowers)

From the navy dotted, cut:
* two 10" squares (outer flowers)

From the navy print, cut:
* two 10" x 14" rectangles (inner leaves)

From the navy solid, cut:
* two 10" x 14" rectangles (outer leaves)

From the fusible fleece, cut:
* two 4½" x 6½" rectangles (leaf blocks)
* two 3" x 17" strips (handle)
* two 5" circles (flowers)

From the fusible web, cut:
* two 3" x 10" strips (handle)

Assembly

1. Prepare two medium octagon flowers from the navy dotted and gold print fabrics, as instructed on pages 19-20.
2. Prepare two 5" x 7" two-leaf blocks from the navy solid and navy print fabrics, as instructed on page 22.

Assemble two medium octagon flowers.

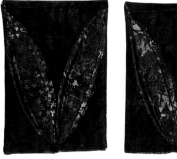

Assemble two leaf units.

For the handle:

1. Prepare the tiny tote handle template, page 127.
2. Stack the inner and outer 17½" fabric strips.
3. Place the handle template on the 17½" fabric strips so that the center is at one end of the fabric strips, as shown.
4. Using a ruler and rotary cutter, cut along the narrow and curved sections of the template, rolling freehand along the curves.
5. Cut the handle template along the dotted lines.
6. Place this smaller template on the two fleece strips, with the center narrow edge on one cut end of the fleece.

Place template on fabric.

Cut fabric.

7. Using a ruler and rotary cutter, cut the fleece along the narrow/curved sections of the template, rolling freehand along the curves.

8. Place the fusible side of the fleece on the wrong side of the flower print fabric strip and fuse.

9. With right sides together, layer an inner gold and an outer large-flower print handle piece.

10. Stitch ¼" from the edge just in the top narrow/curved section, leaving the end unsewn.

11. Clip the curves and turn right-side out, as shown at right.

12. Repeat steps 8 through 11 for the second handle section.

13. Place a 3" x 10" strip of fusible web onto the lining side of the handle, as shown at right, and fuse it according to manufacturer's instructions. Repeat for the second handle.

Place fleece and stitch the seam.

Turn right-side out.

Insert fusible web.

14. Join the handle at the wide end (center bottom) by placing the right sides of the two pieces together and stitching a ¼" seam, as shown below.

Join the center bottom.

15. Zigzag the raw edges of the seam and along the raw edges of the handle.

16. At the narrow end of the handle (center top), match the right sides of just the outer flower fabric and stitch a ¼" seam, as shown at right.

17. On the inside, fold over and overlap the ends and topstitch through all layers.

18. Topstitch ¼" on the finished sides, along the narrow/curved sections of the handle, as shown.

Join the top of the handle.

Join the top of the handle.

For the tote:

1. With right sides together, match the center of one leaf block to the center bottom of the handle, as shown at right, and pin in the center and at the corners.

2. Stitch ¼" seam allowance from the upper right corner, along the side, to the bottom right, along the bottom, and up to the upper left corner. Back-tack at the beginning and the end.

3. Mark the center and corners on the opposite side of the handle.

4. Match the second leaf block to the center and the corners and pin at these points.

5. Stitch ¼" around the right, lower, and left sides of the leaf block, back-tacking at the beginning and the end.

6. Turn the bag right-side out.

7. Place one flower block onto each of the leaf blocks, matching the flower corner to the corner of the handle (above the edge of the leaf unit), as shown at right, and pin in place.

8. Turn the bag inside out and topstitch along the edge of five corners of the flower, back-tacking at the beginning and the end. Start at one corner, stitch to the middle, and stop. Then, start again at the opposite corner.

9. Repeat step 8 for the second flower.

10. Turn the bag right-side out.

11. Apply the hook-and-loop closure to the top inner edges of the two flowers.

Match the centers of leaf unit and the handle.

Stitch the handle to the leaf unit.

Pin the back unit to the handle.

Turn right side out.

Attach the flower unit to the leaf unit.

Topstitch.

Turn right-side out.

Backpack

Y ou'll make a great impression with your young friends with this clever bag. Because it's not gender-specific, make one for the boys in your life from denim or corduroy. Dress it up with trims for a little girl. Made with sophisticated batiks, it will be a fashion statement.

Finished Size

10" x 13" x 2"

Fabric and Notions

* 1 yard dark blue
* ⅜-yard light blue
* ⅜-yard dark green
* ⅜-yard light green print
* ½-yard fusible fleece
* ½-yard fusible web
* 1" strip hook-and-loop tape

Template

Triangle template,
page 115 (T-1)

Completed backpack.

Cutting Plan

From the dark blue, cut:
* one 12" square (large triangle)
* one 10½" x 13½" rectangle (inside of leaf)
* two 15" x 15½" rectangles (back)
* one 1½" x 15½" strip (back binding)
* two 4" x 32" strips (straps)
* one 4" x 12" strip (handle)

From the light blue, cut:
* one 12" square (large triangle)
* one 10½" x 13½" rectangle (front of leaf)

From the dark green, cut:
* one 10½" x 13½" rectangle (inner leaf)

From the light green print, cut:
* one 10½" x 13½" rectangle
  (inside of leaf)

From the fusible fleece, cut:
* one 10" x 13" rectangle (leaf)
* one 5" x 10" rectangle (triangle)
* one 15" square (back)
* two 1" x 32" strips (straps)
* one 1" x 12" strip (handle)

From the fusible web, cut:
* one 15" square (back)

Assembly

Note: Because of its large size, the leaf unit is made from seamed, rather than single, pieces. Follow these special instructions:

1. With right sides out, layer the dark green and the light blue rectangles. The top layer of the leaf will be cut into triangles.

2. Find the center bottom by folding the pieces in half and finger-press.

3. Cut from the center fold to the upper right corner, and then cut from the upper left corner to the fold, as shown above.

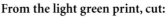

Layer the rectangles.

Cut center triangle.

4. With right sides out, place the dark blue lining rectangle on the light green print rectangle.

5. Place the two center triangle pieces from step 3 so that the light blue triangle is right-side down on the dark blue rectangle. Pin.

6. Stitch ¼" seam allowance across the top of the triangle.

Layer the triangles right-side down on the rectangles and stitch across the top.

7. Turn right-side out.

8. Center the 10" x 13" rectangle of fleece between the dark blue and the green print layers.

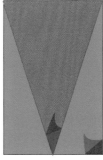

Turn right-side out.　　Insert fleece rectangle.

(continued)

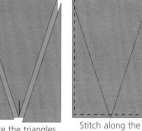

9. With the light blue facing up, place the remaining right triangles on the green print rectangle and pin.

Replace the triangles.

Stitch along the raw edges.

10. Stitch along the raw edges.

11. Turn back and topstitch the leaf petals, as shown.

12. Place lines of quilt stitching to "echo" the outline of the leaf shapes.

Turn back and top-stitch the petals.

Completed leaf unit.

For the back:

1. Orient the dark blue rectangle so that the shorter side is the width.

2. With the dark blue 15"-wide by 15½"-tall rectangles right sides out, insert the 15" square of fleece between the layers, so that it aligns with the top edge of the rectangles. Press to fuse.

3. Insert the 15" square of fusible web on the non-fused side and press to fuse.

4. Cut a 2½" square from the two lower corners of the back piece.

5. Quilt the back side with several rows of stitching.

Stitch quilting lines.

Insert fleece and cut away lower corners.

Quilt the back layers.

For the binding, handle, and straps:

1. Prepare the binding strip, the handle, and the straps, as instructed on pages 34-35.

2. Place the straps on the outside of the back piece, as shown at right, pin, and secure the straps with basting stitches.

3. Wrap the binding over the upper raw edge of the back section.

Place the straps on the back and wrap the top with binding.

4. Stitch the binding through all layers.

For the final assembly:

1. With right sides together, match the leaf unit to the back piece, as shown at right, and pin.

2. Stitch with a ¼" seam allowance along the side seam and then zigzag over the edge of the seam allowance.

3. Repeat steps 1 and 2 for the remaining side seam.

4. With right sides together, match the two short sections at the bottom of the back piece (with the straps basted in between) to form the corner. Pin.

5. Stitch with a ¼" seam allowance, as shown, back-tacking at the inner corner.

6. Repeat steps 4 and 5 for the remaining corner.

7. With the right sides together, match the front lower edge of the leaf block to the lower edge of the back section and pin.

8. Stitch with a ¼" seam allowance and turn the bag right-side out.

9. Place the handle at the top edge of the back section, as shown far right, and pin.

10. Prepare one large triangle unit, as instructed on page 24.

11. Place the large triangle unit over the top edge of the back section and over the ends of the handle and pin.

12. Topstitch at the edge of the triangle unit, as shown, back-tacking at the start and end of the stitching line.

13. Apply the hook-and-loop tape to the inside of the triangle at the point matching it to the front of the leaf.

Match the leaf unit to the back.

Stitch the corners.

Turn right-side out.

Assemble a large triangle unit.

Place the handle at the center back.

Attach the triangle.

Topstitch the backpack.

Pyramid Bag

This bag may have magical powers for the fashion-conscious. Nothing short of an attention-getter, it will be the hit of the party scene, as it's perfect for the necessities. Or for a home decorating twist, hang bunches on your holiday tree that are filled with gifts and goodies.

Finished Size

8½" x 8½" x 10"

Fabric and Notions

* ½-yard gold
* ½-yard pink
* ⅓-yard fusible fleece
* 7" zipper

Templates

* Large triangle template*, page 115 (T-1)
* Fleece, page 116 (T-2)

*Note the special template preparation instructions that result in a hexagon-shaped template.

Cutting Plan

From the gold, cut:
* four bias-edged hexagons (inside)

From the pink, cut:
* four bias-edged hexagons (outside)
* one 3" x 16" strip (handle)

From the fleece, cut:
* one 5"-wide strip (cut into four triangles with the T-2 template)
* one 1" x 16" strip (handle)

Assembly

1. With the pink fabric outside and the gold inside, prepare four triangle flower units, as instructed on page 24.

Assemble the triangle units.

2. Insert the zipper between two of the triangles, as shown below.

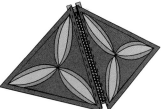

Insert zipper.

3. With right sides out, stitch a third triangle onto one of the paired triangles, as shown below.

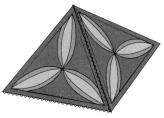

Add third triangle.

4. With right sides out, pin the fourth triangle to the joined triangles. This unit will draw the blocks into the pyramid shape.

5. Zigzag stitch around the fourth triangle, as shown below.

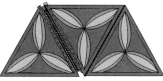

Zigzag around fourth triangle.

6. Stitch the final seam on the right side.

7. Attach the handle to the outside, as instructed on page 35.

Purple variation.

Notice how changing fabric colors can create several different looks.

Jewel Box Bag

The name of this bag was inspired by the grand crystal palace from the St. Louis World's Fair. It's an all-glass building with many faceted design elements. The bag is reminiscent of the faceted glass boxes used to keep precious jewels. Dressed up in silky fabric, this little bag will protect your gems.

Finished Size

6" x 6" x 8" [5" x 5" x 7"]*

*Measurements for the smaller bag
appear in brackets.

Fabric and Notions

* ⅔-yard [⅔-yard] check
* ⅔-yard [⅔-yard] plaid
* ⅓-yard fusible fleece
* 7" [7"] zipper

Template

Medium or small triangle
template*, page 119 (T-5)

*Note the special template
preparation instructions
that result in a hexagon-shaped
template.

Cutting Plan

From the check, cut:
* three 12" x 16" [10" x 14"] rectangles (outside)
* two medium [small] bias-edged hexagons (hexagons are
  folded to create triangle ends)
* two 2½" x 14" [2½" x 14"] strips (handles)

From the plaid, cut:
* three 12" x 16" (10" x 14") rectangles (sides)
* two medium [small] bias-edged hexagons (triangle ends)

From the fusible fleece, cut:
* two ¾" x 14" strip (handles)

Assembly

1. Prepare three 6" x 8" [5" x 7"] rectangle
   units, as instructed on page 26.

2. With the hexagon-shaped cutouts,
   prepare two medium [small] triangle
   units, as instructed on page 24.

Assemble rectangle
and triangle units.

3. Insert the zipper between two of
   the rectangles, as shown below.

Insert zipper.

4. With zigzag stitching, join the third
   rectangle to the pair, as shown.

Add third
rectangle.

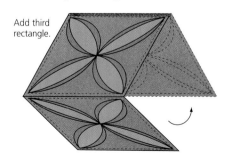

5. With right sides out and matching
   the corners, join a triangle to one
   end of the rectangle units, as shown
   below.

Join first triangle.

6. Repeat step 5 for the other end.

7. Stitch the remaining seam, joining
   the rectangles.

8. Prepare handles, as instructed on
   pages 34-35.

9. Position, pin, and stitch handles to
   the outside of the bag.

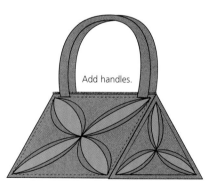

Add handles.

Citrus Slice Purse

These whip up so fast, you can fill a fruit bowl and maybe a vegetable medley, too. Quickly make one easy block, add a zipper, and you're done. Make a miniature version to carry your change, as detailed in the next project, page 73.

Finished Size

5" x 10" x ½"

Fabric and Notions

✳ ⅝-yard yellow
✳ ⅝-yard green
✳ ⅓-yard fusible fleece
✳ 9" zipper

Templates

✳ Sunflower template, page 124 (T-10)
✳ Fleece template, page 125 (T-11)
✳ 10" circle template, page 126 (T-12)

Cutting Plan

From the yellow, cut:
✳ one 22" square (sunflower)
✳ one 1½"-wide bias strip (binding)

From the green, cut:
✳ one 22" square (sunflower)
✳ one sunflower shape (pocket)

From the fusible fleece, cut:
✳ one 10" circle (sunflower)

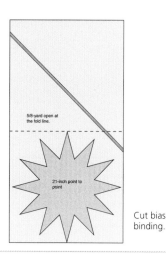

5/8-yard open at the fold line.

21-inch point to point

Cut bias binding.

Assembly

1. Prepare one sunflower unit, as instructed on page 21.

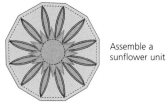

Assemble a sunflower unit.

2. Cut the sunflower unit in half, as shown below.

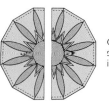

Cut the sunflower in half.

3. Cover the raw edges of both sunflower halves with the bias binding, as shown.

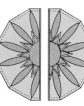

Bind the raw edges of the halves.

4. Insert the zipper between the two sunflower halves, pin, and topstitch in place.

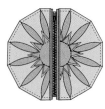

Insert the zipper between the halves.

5. Fold the pocket in half.

6. Place the pocket on the inside of one sunflower half, as shown below, and pin in place.

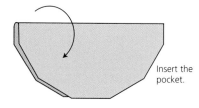

Insert the pocket.

7. With right sides out, pin the sunflower halves together, catching the pocket in the pins.

8. Stitch ¼" from the outer edge.

9. Cover the outer edges with double-fold bias binding.

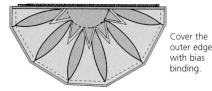

Cover the outer edge with bias binding.

For the handle:

1. Topstitch in the center of an 18" double-fold bias binding.

2. Slip the two raw ends of the handle between the zipper and the joined sunflowers and stitch in place.

Insert the handle between the end of the zipper and the binding.

Mini Coin Purse

I t's a tiny version of the citrus slice and it holds just enough money to buy a coffee while on break. Tuck it in your jeans pocket. Stuff it in a Christmas stocking or tie it on a gift for a special treat.

Finished Size

2¾" x 5" x ⅛"

Fabric and Notions

* ¼-yard light check
* ¼-yard medium check
* 1 yard bias tape
* 4" zipper

Template

Small octagon flower template, page 123 (T-9)

Cutting Plan

From the light check, cut:
* one 9" square (small octagon flower)

From the medium check, cut:
* one 9" square (small octagon flower)

Assembly

1. Prepare one small octagon flower unit cut from the two 9" squares, as instructed on pages 19-20.

2. Complete steps 2 through 4 and 7 through 9 from the Citrus Slice Purse instructions on the facing page.

Finished coin purse.

Grandma's Not-a-Square Bag

My friend's mom loves animal print bags. She's almost 80, but has a job she loves and is game to learn new skills. While being both a grandma and a great-grandma, she remains in the know. I thought of her when I named this bag. It fits right in with today's fashion-conscious moms and it's big enough to carry all their gear.

Finished Size

11" x 11" x 4"

Fabric and Notions

* ¾-yard light green
* ⅜-yard yellow
* ⅝-yard navy
* ¾-yard lilac batik
* 14" zipper

Template

None needed. A 12½" rotary ruler is just the right size to cut the square.

Cutting Plan

From the light green, cut:
* two 10½" squares (folded petals)
* two 8" x 22" rectangles (side rectangles)
* one 4½"-wide selvedge-to-selvedge strip, cut in half (handles)

From the yellow, cut:
* two 12½" squares (inside of the squares)
* two 4½" x 11" rectangles (bottom)

From the navy, cut:
* two 10½" squares (folded petals)
* two 8" x 22" rectangles (side rectangles)

From the lilac batik, cut:
* two 12½" squares (inner front squares)
* two 4" x 11" rectangles (side piece inserts)

Assembly

1. Prepare two modular squares, as instructed on page 26.

2. Follow the mirror leaf instructions on page 23 to prepare two 4" x 11" side rectangles, but place one 4" x 11" lilac batik rectangle right-side up inside the folded flaps after step 5. Complete the remaining instructions.

3. Prepare the bottom piece, as instructed on pages 35-36.

4. Place the zipper between the two squares, as shown at right, so that one end is even with the corner. Pin in place and topstitch.

5. Open the zipper.

6. With right sides together, match one rectangle unit to the side of one square, pin, and stitch ⅛" seam allowance to join the units. Repeat for the second side, as shown below.

(continued)

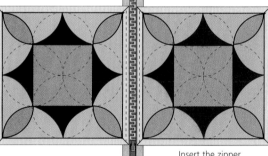

Assemble the modular squares and side rectangle units.

Insert the zipper between the squares.

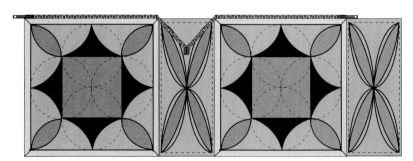

Join the side rectangles.

7. With right sides together, match the center of the bottom piece to the center of one modular square unit, as shown below, and pin at the center and the corners.

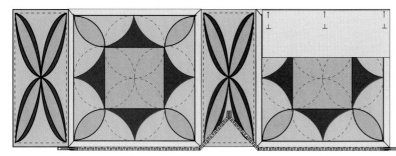

Match the center of the bottom to the joined units and pin in place.

8. Stitch ⅛" seam allowance around the bottom piece, carefully turning the corners.

9. With the bag inside-out, join the remaining seam with an ⅛" seam allowance.

10. Turn right-side out.

Join units to the bottom.

Bag without handles.

11. Prepare the handles, as instructed on pages 34-35.

12. Attach the handles to the top area of the bag, as instructed on page 35.

Take a walk on the wild side with this variation that uses a jungle print to create an entirely new look.

Hatbox Bag

S tuff this clever bag with all your necessities. There's plenty of room for a clutch, makeup, and keys. It's handy for travel as a cosmetic case.

Finished Size

10" x10" x 4"

Fabric and Notions

* ⅝-yard light blue
* ⅝-yard dark blue
* ⅝-yard light green
* ½-yard yellow
* ½-yard fusible fleece
* 4½" x 17" rectangle fusible web
* 12" zipper

Templates

* Large octagon flower template, page 120 (T-6)
* Fleece template, page 121 (T-7)

A yellow variation for the Hatbox Bag.

Cutting Plan

From the light blue, cut:
* two 22" squares
  (insides of octagon flowers)

From the dark blue, cut:
* one 22" square
  (outside of one octagon flower)

From the light green, cut:
* one 22" square
  (outside of one octagon flower)

From the yellow, cut:
* two 5" x 14" rectangles
  (zipper assembly)
* two 4½" x 5" rectangles
  (zipper ends)
* two 4½" x 17" rectangles (bottom)
* two 4" x 18" strips (handles)
* one octagon (optional pocket)

✳ Laura's Hint

Cut a 1" selvedge-to-selvedge fleece strip in half for the handles.

From the fusible fleece, cut:
* two 10" circles fleece
  (large flower units)
* one 3¾" x 17" rectangle fleece
  (bottom)
* two 1¾" x 13" rectangles
  (zipper assembly)
* two 2" x 4" rectangles (zipper ends)
* two 1" x 21" strips fleece (handles)

From the fusible web, cut:
* one 4½" x 17" rectangle fusible web
  (bottom)

Assembly

1. Prepare two large octagon flower units with the light blue fabric inside as instructed on pages 19-20.

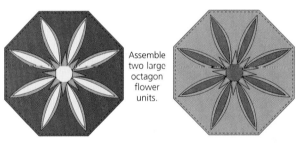

Assemble two large octagon flower units.

2. Optional: Add a pocket to the inside of one of the flowers, as follows:

   a. Prepare the octagon fleece, using the template on page 121.

   b. Cut one octagon-shape for the pocket.

   c. Fold the octagon-shaped fabric in half and press.

   d. Place the folded pocket on the inside of the second flower unit and pin.

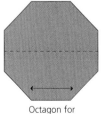

Octagon for the pocket.

Fold to form the pocket.

Place the pocket on the inside of the second flower unit.

3. Prepare the zipper assembly by folding the 5" x 14" yellow rectangles in half lengthwise and insert the zipper, as shown at right.

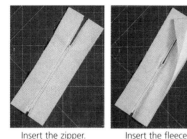

Insert the zipper.   Insert the fleece.

4. Layer the fleece rectangles between the folds.

5. Fold the 4½" x 5" rectangles in half to measure 2½" x 4½".

6. Place these folded rectangles over the ends of the zipper, as shown at right. Pin in place and stitch along the folds.

Place the rectangles over the ends of the zipper.

7. Prepare the bottom, as instructed on page 35-36.

8. Join the bottom to the zipper assembly on one short end, as shown below.

Joining the zipper assembly.

For joining the flowers to the zipper assembly:

1. With right sides together, match the center of the zipper with the center of one large octagon flower unit and pin in place.

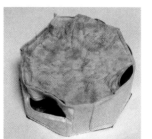

Match the centers and pin.

2. Pin the corners of the flower unit to the zipper assembly.

3. Stitch a ¼" seam allowance along the edge of the flower unit, as shown below right.

Pin the flower corners to the zipper assembly.

Stitch around the octagon.

4. Join the zipper assembly seam to form a circle.

5. Insert pins on the unfinished side of the zipper assembly at the corners formed by the first flower unit and open the zipper.

Join the zipper assembly.

6. With right sides together, match the second flower unit, with the optional flower unit at the bottom, to the corners of the zipper assembly and pin in place.

Match the second flower to the zipper assembly.

The pocket is formed at the bottom of the bag.

Stitch around the second flower unit.

7. Stitch ¼" along the sides of the second flower unit.

Turn right-side out.

8. Turn the bag right-side out through the zipper opening.

For the handles:

1. Prepare the handles, as instructed on pages 34-35.

2. Place the handles on the outside of the bag, as shown at right, and pin.

3. Stitch the handles to the bag.

Place the handles on the bag.

Hatbox Bag 79

Barrel Bag

A s is true of the Hatbox Bag, pages 77-79, the barrel bag has multiple uses. It, too, is large enough to hold a clutch, makeup, and keys. Or it may be used as a cosmetic case.

A variation in color for the Barrel Bag.

Finished Size

6" x 6½" x 10"

Fabric and Notions

* 1 yard dark blue
* ⅜-yard light blue
* ½-yard light green
* ¼-yard batting
* ½-yard fusible fleece
* 9" zipper

Templates

* Small octagon flower template, page 123 (T-9)
* Medium octagon flower template, page 122 (T-8)
* 4" and 6" circle templates, page 126 (T-12)

Cutting Plan

From the dark blue, cut:
* two 8½" squares (small octagon flower unit)
* two 12½" squares (medium octagon flower units)
* four 10" x 15" rectangles (outer layers of leaf units)
* two 5" x 10" rectangles (bottom)
* two 4" x 21" rectangles (handles)

From the light blue, cut:
* two 8½" squares (small octagon flower units)
* two 12½" squares (medium octagon flower units)

From the light green, cut:
* four 10" x 15" rectangles (inner layers of leaf units)

＊ Laura's Hint

Cut a 1" selvedge-to-selvedge fleece strip in half for the handles.

From the batting, cut:
* two 4" circles batting (small flower units)

From the fusible fleece, cut:
* two 6" circles fleece (medium flower units)
* four 4¾" x 7¼" fleece rectangles (leaf units)
* one 4¾" x 9" fleece rectangle (bottom)
* two 1" x 21" fleece strips (handles)

From the fusible web, cut:
* one 4¾" x 9½" rectangle fusible web (bottom)

Assembly

1. Prepare two small and two medium octagon flower units, as instructed on pages 19-20.

2. Prepare four two-leaf units, as instructed on page 22.

Assemble two small flower units, two medium flower units, and four two-leaf units.

3. Combine two two-leaf units with a small flower unit. Repeat with the remaining small flower and two-leaf units.

Combine the leaf and flower units.

4. Center the zipper between the two flower-leaf units, pin, and topstitch along the fold.

5. Prepare the bottom, as on pages 35-36.

6. With right sides together, join one side of the bottom section, using a ¼" seam allowance, to the previously joined combination blocks, as shown at right.

Insert the zipper.

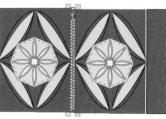

Join the bottom section.

7. Cut between two alternate points, as shown at right, to adjust the medium flower units so the bottom of the bag lays flat.

8. Match one medium flower right sides together, so the top center point of the flower is at the center of the main body of the bag, as shown, and pin in place.

9. Pin the remaining corners to the bag.

10. Stitch a ¼" seam allowance around the flower.

11. Repeat steps 8 through 10 for remaining side.

12. With the bag inside-out and the zipper open, stitch the remaining seam between the bottom and the combined section.

13. Turn right-side out.

14. Prepare the handles, as instructed on pages 34-35.

15. Place the handles on the outside of the bag, pin, and stitch in place.

Cut the flower unit to flatten it by skipping one point.

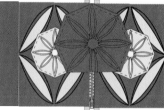

Match the upper center of the flower to the zipper.

Completed bag inside-out.

Finished bag.

Little Zippy Tote

With the surge in cell phone and digital camera use, it seemed natural to design a bag to secure such items in this handy-sized zipper tote. There's also an inside pocket under the flower to stow valuables.

Finished Size

5" x 8" x 3"

Fabric and Notions

* ⅝-yard dark green batik
* ½-yard light green batik
* ¼-yard pink batik
* 6" circle batting
* ⅓-yard fusible fleece
* 2¾" x 13" rectangle fusible web
* 12" zipper
* 1" strip hook-and-loop tape

Template

Small octagon flower template, page 123 (T-9)

Cutting Plan

From the dark green batik, cut:
* one 11" x 15" rectangle (mirror leaf unit)
* one 10½" x 14½" rectangle (basic leaf unit)
* two 3" x 14" rectangles (zipper section)
* two 3½" x 14" rectangles (sides/bottom section)
* one 8½" square (small octagon flower)
* two 4" x 13" strips (handles)

From the light green batik, cut:
* one 11" x 15" rectangle (mirror leaf unit)
* one 10½" x 14½" rectangle (basic leaf unit)
* one 5½" x 15" rectangle (pocket)

From the pink batik, cut:
* one 8½" square (small octagon flower)

From the batting, cut:
* one 4" circle batting (small flower unit)

From the fleece, cut:
* two 4¾" x 6¾" fleece rectangles (leaf units)
* one 5" x 7" rectangle (pocket)
* two 1" x 14" rectangles (zipper section)
* one 2¾" x 13" rectangle fleece (side/bottom section)
* two 1" x 13" fleece strips (handles)

From the fusible web, cut:
* one 2¾" x 13" rectangle fusible web (side/bottom section)

Assembly

1. Prepare the small octagon flower unit, as instructed on pages 19-20.

Assemble one small octagon flower.

2. Prepare the basic leaf unit, as instructed on page 22.

3. Prepare the mirror leaf unit, as instructed on page 23.

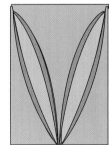

Assemble one basic leaf unit.

Assemble one mirror leaf unit.

4. Fold the 5½" x 15" rectangle in half to make a 5½" x 7½" rectangle for the pocket.

5. Insert the 5" x 7" rectangle of fleece between the layers of the rectangle pocket piece, as shown, and fuse.

Insert the fleece between the folded layers.

6. Zigzag stitch over the three unfinished sides.

7. With its right side up and the fold of the pocket section toward the top, center the basic leaf unit on the pocket section, with the bottoms of both units even.

8. Topstitch the leaf unit onto the pocket section, as shown at right.

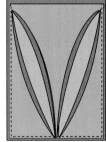

Topstitch the leaf unit to the pocket.

(continued)

For the zipper section:

1. With right sides out, fold the two 3" x 14" dark green rectangles in half lengthwise.

2. Insert the zipper between the folds, pin, and topstitch.

3. Insert the 1" x 14" fleece rectangles between the folds and press to fuse.

4. Prepare the side/ bottom section, as instructed on page 35-36.

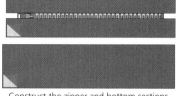

Construct the zipper and bottom sections.

5. Join one side of the side/bottom section to the zipper section, as shown below.

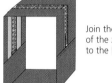

Join the zipper section to the side/bottom.

6. Join the side/bottom section to the zipper section with a basting stitch to make a continuous loop, as shown.

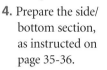

Join the second end of the zipper section to the bottom.

7. With right sides together, match the top center of the basic leaf unit to the top center of the side/bottom section.

Match the center of the basic leaf unit to the center of the zipper assembly.

8. Make any adjustments to the size of the loop, pin, and stitch the loop.

9. Stitch a ¼" seam allowance around all four sides.

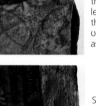

Stitch the loop.

Sew the front to the side/bottom.

10. Open the zipper.

11. Mark the corners and the centers with pins on the opposite edges of the side/bottom section.

Pin the centers and the corners.

12. With right sides together, match the mirror leaf unit to the side/bottom section and stitch ¼" seam allowance around all four sides.

13. Turn the body piece right-side out.

Stitch around all four sides.

For the handles:

1. Prepare the handles, as instructed on pages 34-35.

2. Pin the handles to the side section near the zipper, as shown.

3. Topstitch the handles to secure.

Pin the handles below the zipper.

4. Center the octagon flower over the front leaf unit, pin, and topstitch the flower to the top section of the body near the zipper.

5. Attach the hook-and-loop tape to the underside of the flower and the top of the leaf unit, as shown below.

Topstitch the handles.

Attach the hook-and-loop tape.

6. Refold the flower over the pocket.

Completed bag.

3 Blooming Flowers for the Home

I n addition to large quilts, this chapter contains a series of projects that can be completed in a day's time. The accents for your home include wall hangings, table covers, bathmats, and a pillow.

Four-Flower Wall Hanging

Four flowers make this wall hanging bloom. Bring your garden inside by hanging this bouquet for a touch of spring all year long.

Finished Size

20" square

Fabric and Notions

* 1¼ yards green batik
* 1⅝ yards pink batik

Template

Large octagon flower template, page 120 (T-6)

✳ Laura's Hint

To hang this project after it's done, attach loops of ribbon with pins to the back side.

Cutting Plan

From the green batik, cut:
✳ four 22" squares (octagon flowers)
✳ three 9½" bias squares (leaf units)

✳ three 1¾" selvedge-to-selvedge strips (binding)

From the pink batik, cut:
✳ four 22" squares (octagon flowers)
✳ three 9½" bias squares (leaf units)

Assembly

1. Prepare four large octagon flowers, as instructed on pages 19-20.

2. Prepare three leaf squares, as instructed on page 22.

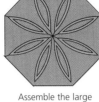

Assemble the large octagon flower units.

Assemble three leaf squares.

Cut two of the leaf squares in half diagonally.

3. Cut two of the leaf squares in half diagonally.

4. Join the four octagons.

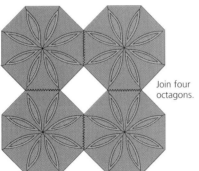

Join four octagons.

For the patches:

1. Place one whole leaf square in the center and the half-squares along the sides, as shown.

2. Join the patches, as instructed on page 16.

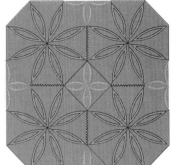

Join the patches.

For the binding:

1. Join the three 1¾" strips and bind, as instructed on pages 16-17.

Finished wall hanging.

Arrange patches.

Four-Flower Pillow

With a simple addition of a pocket, the Wall Hanging project, pages 86 and 87, becomes a throw pillow. Use one or more to decorate your home with lush florals. Add the designer's touch.

Finished Size

20" square

Fabric and Notions

* 2⅛ yards green batik
* 1⅜ yards pink batik
* 20" square pillow form

Template

Large octagon flower template, page 120 (T-6)

Cutting Plan

From the green batik, cut:
* four 22" squares (octagon flowers)
* three 9½" bias squares (leaf units)
* two 15" x 21" rectangles (back pocket)

From the pink batik, cut:
* four 22" squares (octagon flowers)
* three 9½" bias squares (leaf units)

Assembly

1. Complete the wall hanging assembly steps 1 through 4 as well as the patch insertion steps 1 and 2, as instructed on page 87.
2. Fold one side of a back pocket rectangle so that it measures 13" x 21" and pin.
3. Stitch along both the fold and the raw edge.

4. Repeat steps 2 and 3 for the other rectangle.
5. With the right sides together, layer the back pocket rectangles on the front flower piece, so that the folds are in the center and overlap, as shown. Pin.
6. Trim the extra fabric at the corners.
7. Stitch a ½" seam allowance around all four sides and across the corners.
8. Turn right-side out, insert a pillow form or folded batting through the overlapped opening.

Layer the back pieces.

Trim the corners and stitch around the outside.

Four-Square Pillow

P illows are an extremely popular trend in home décor. This particular pillow
is a larger version of the Four-Square Tote project (pages 51 and 52) with
a pocket in the back. Because it's made with just four basic squares, it's quick
to complete.

Finished Size

17" square

Fabric and Notions

* ⅝-yard blue-and-yellow check
* ⅝-yard yellow check
* 1 yard dark blue check
* 2 yards navy single-fold wide bias tape
* 18" square pillow form

Template

None needed. A 12½" rotary ruler is just the right size to cut the square.

Cutting Plan

From the blue-and-yellow check, cut:
* three 12½" bias-cut squares (front)

From the yellow check, cut:
* three 12½" bias-cut squares (front)

From the dark blue check, cut:
* two 12½" bias-cut squares (front)
* two 12" x 18" rectangles (back side)

Assembly

1. Mixing the colors, prepare the four basic squares and assemble them as instructed in steps 2 through 6 in the Four-Square Tote project (page 52).

2. Fold one side of a back side rectangle, so that it measures 10" x 18" and pin.

3. Stitch along the fold and along the raw edge.

4. Repeat steps 2 and 3 for the remaining rectangle.

5. With the right sides out, layer the back side rectangles on the back of the flower piece, so that the folds are in the center and overlap, as shown below. Pin.

Layer the back rectangles to the back of the flower piece.

6. Wrap the bias tape over the edges of the front and back pieces and pin.

7. Stitch ¼" through the bias tape around all four sides.

8. Insert a pillow form (or folded batting) through the overlapped opening, as shown below, and stitch opening shut.

Insert the pillow form through the opening in the back.

Front of pillow.

Diamond Placemats

F ive diamond units merge into clever placemats. Alternating lights and darks make for delightful effects. For a different design, make these in bright colors for a sparkling table setting. They're quick and easy and make wonderful gifts.

Finished Size

11½" x 20"

Fabric and Notions

* 2 yards* navy homespun
* 2 yards* blue check homespun
* 1½ yards* navy
   single-fold bias tape

*Enough to complete
   a set of four placemats.

Templates

Large diamond template,
page 117 (T-3)

* Laura's Hint

*To make coordinating
coasters like those shown
in the project photo on
the previous page,
use the leftover fabric
to create basic squares,
as instructed on page 25.*

Cutting Plan

From the navy homespun, cut:
* 20 large diamonds (diamonds)

From the blue check homespun, cut:
* 20 large diamonds (diamonds)

Assembly

1. Prepare five large diamond units per placemat, as instructed on page 29.
2. Alternate the light and dark fabrics as desired, as shown.

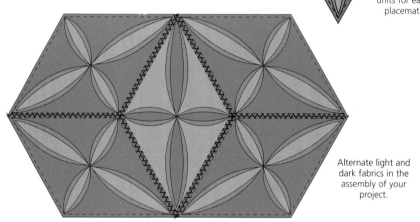

Assemble five
large diamond
units for each
placemat.

Alternate light and
dark fabrics in the
assembly of your
project.

3. Join the large diamonds with zigzag stitching in the pattern shown.
4. Bind with the single-fold bias binding.

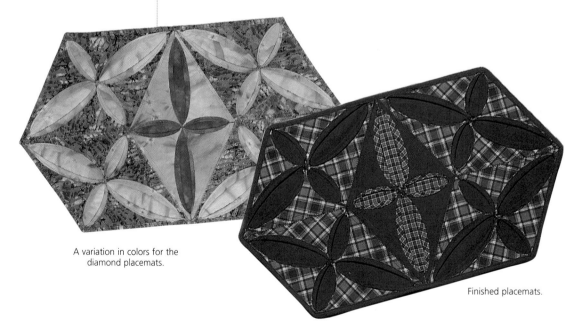

A variation in colors for the
diamond placemats.

Finished placemats.

Rectangle Placemats and Coasters Set

These placemats are made from layered fabrics that are peeled back and bent into curvy designs. Each mat is a modular rectangle block. Play with value and color for negative/positive image effects.

Finished Size

11¾" x 17" (placemats);
4" square (coasters)

Fabric and Notions

* 1 yard* pink check
* 1 yard* pink print
* 1 yard* large green check
* 1 yard* small green check
* 1 yard* fusible fleece

*Enough to complete
  a set of four placemats.

Template

None needed.

Cutting Plan

From the pink check, cut:
* four 13½" x 19½" rectangles (back)

From the pink print, cut:
* four 13½" x 19½" rectangles (front)

From the large green check, cut:
* four 11¾" x 17¼" rectangles (front)

From the small green check, cut:
* four 11¾" x 17¾" rectangles (front)

From the fusible fleece, cut:
* four 12" x 17" rectangles

Assembly

1. Prepare one modular rectangle for each placemat, as instructed on page 27.

For the coasters:

These are peek-a-boo squares.

1. Cut four 6" bias squares from the left-over green print and check fabric and four 3¾" straight-grain squares pink print.

2. Prepare basic squares "peek-a-boo" version, as instructed on page 25, with a pink-print accent square inserted after step 4.

3. Refold and stitch as instructed in the remaining steps of the basic square instructions.

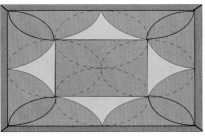

Assemble modular rectangle.

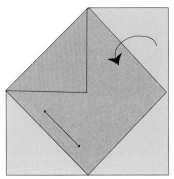

Fold the corners to center.

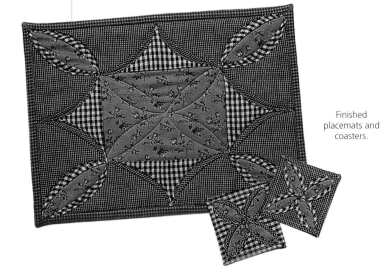

Finished
placemats and
coasters.

Hexagon Bathmat

The series of bathmats was inspired when I saw one of my ragged-edge flower quilts lying on the floor. It looked like a lily pad. A slight shift in thought sent me to the bathmat concept. With just seven flowers, you'll have this done in no time. Sink your wet feet into its fuzzy flowers. Hang it up to dry.

Finished Size

30" x 30"

Fabric* and Notions

* 2½ yards 45"-wide blue flannel
* 2½ yards 45"-wide white flannel
* 1 yard lightweight batting
* Fray Check™

*Leave the fabric unlaundered.

Templates

* Hexagon flower template, page 118 (T-4, cut on the black lines)
* Hexagon batting template, page 119 (T-5, cut on the black lines)
* Small diamond template, page 117 (T-3, cut on the red lines)
* Small diamond fleece template, page 118 (T-4, cut on the red lines)

Finished bathmat.

Cutting Plan

From the blue flannel, cut:
* seven 22" squares (hexagon flowers)
* three small diamonds
* four 1" x 30" bias strips, as shown in the diagram (binding)

From the white flannel, cut:
* seven 22" squares (hexagon flowers)
* three small diamonds

From the batting, cut:
* seven hexagons (center)
* three small diamonds (patches)

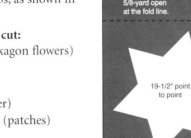

Each strip yields about 30"

5/8-yard open at the fold line.

19-1/2" point to point

Cut the bias binding.

Assembly

1. Prepare seven hexagon flowers, as instructed on page 17.

Assemble seven hexagon flower units.

2. Prepare three small diamonds for patches, as instructed on page 29.

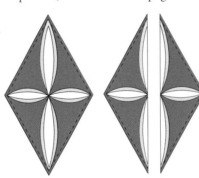

Assemble three diamond patches.

Cut the diamonds in half vertically.

3. Cut all three diamonds in half vertically, as shown above right.

4. Join the seven hexagon flowers, as shown.

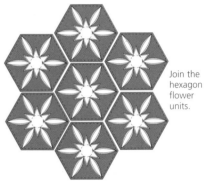

Join the hexagon flower units.

5. Insert the half-diamonds in the gaps formed by the joined flower units.

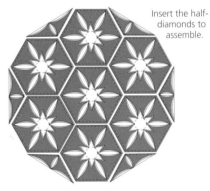

Insert the half-diamonds to assemble.

6. Bind, as instructed for raw edge binding on pages 16-17.

7. Launder with mild soap and machine dry.

Octagon Bathmat

Once you've sunk your toes into this snuggly mat, you'll want to make one for every season. It's quick to make from eight octagon flowers and nine square fillers. Make several and rotate them through the laundry. They'll get fluffier, the more they're washed and dried.

Finished Size

34" x 34"

Fabric* and Notions

* 3 yards 45"-wide blue flannel
* 2⅔ yards 45"-wide yellow flannel
* 1 yard lightweight batting
* Fray Check™

*Leave the fabric unlaundered.

Template

* Large octagon flower template, page 120 (T-6)
* Octagon batting template, page 121 (T-7, cut on the black lines)

Cutting Plan

From the blue flannel, cut:
* eight 22" squares (octagon flowers)
* nine 5" bias squares (patches)
* four 1" x 30" bias strips, as illustrated in the diagram (binding)

From the yellow flannel, cut:
* eight 22" squares (octagon flowers)
* nine 5" bias squares (patches)

From the batting, cut:
* eight 10" circles (flowers)
* nine 4" squares (patches)

Each strip yields about 30"

5/8-yard open at the fold line.

21-inch point to point

Cut the bias binding strips.

Assembly

1. Prepare eight octagon flowers, as instructed on pages 19-20.

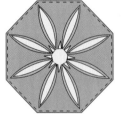

Prepare octagon flowers.

2. Cut four flower units in half, as shown below.

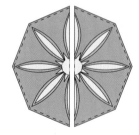

Cut four flower units in half.

3. Prepare 9 bias squares for patches, as instructed on page 30.

Prepare bias squares for patches.

4. Join the four whole flower units with the half-flowers, as shown.

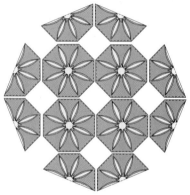

Join the whole and half-flower units.

5. Insert the bias squares in the gaps formed by the joined flower units, as shown below.

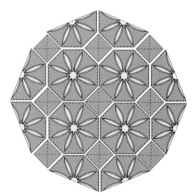

Insert the bias squares to complete assembly.

6. Bind, as instructed for raw edge binding on pages 16-17.

Finished bathmat.

In this view of the back of the bathmat, contrasting patches form a pattern.

This color variation is great for the guys in your house.

Sunflower Bathmat

Use this design when you want the largest bouquet. Seven sunflowers revolve around to make a circle of fluffy warmth for your feet. Made from batiks, this project works equally as well as a table topper.

Finished Size

30" x 30"

Fabric* and Notions

* 2½ yards 45"-wide plaid flannel
* 2½ yards 45"-wide yellow flannel
* 1 yard lightweight batting
* Fray Check™

*Leave the fabric unlaundered.

Templates

* Sunflower template, page 124 (T-10)
* Sunflower batting template, page 125 (T-11, cut on black lines)
* Triangle patch and batting template, page 125 (T-11, cut on red and blue lines)

Cutting Plan

From the plaid flannel, cut:
* seven 22" squares (sunflower units)
* 12 triangles (patches) from the flower unit scraps.
* four 1" x 30" bias strips, as shown in the diagram (binding)

From the yellow flannel, cut:
* seven 22" squares (flowers)
* 12 triangles (patches)

From the batting, cut:
* seven 10" circles (flowers)
* 12 triangles (patches)

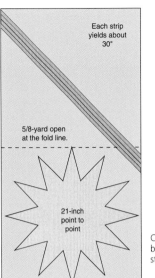

Each strip yields about 30"

5/8-yard open at the fold line.

21-inch point to point

Cut the bias binding strips.

Assembly

1. Prepare seven sunflower units, as instructed on page 21.

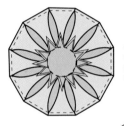

Assemble seven sunflower units.

Assemble 12 triangle units.

2. Prepare 12 triangle patches, as instructed on pages 31-32.

3. Join the seven flower units, as shown.

Join the flower units.

Finished bathmat.

Note the interesting pattern on the back side.

4. Insert the triangles in the gaps formed by the joined flower units, as instructed on page 33.

Insert the triangles to fill the gaps.

5. Bind, as instructed for raw edge binding on pages 16-17.
6. Wash and dry the bathmat. Fluff when dry.

Instead of a bathmat, try this design as a table topper that dresses up the dining room in batik. The instructions are exactly the same as those for the bathmat.

Diamond Illusions Quilt

Using three shades of color develops the tumbling blocks illusion. Depending on the color placement, other effects are possible. Explore the possibilities by rearranging the units and adding different color combinations.

Finished Size

33" x 38"

Fabric and Notions

* 1 yard blue batik
* 1 yard green batik
* 1 yard peach batik
* 1 yard pink batik
* 1 yard beige batik
* 1 yard light green batik
* ⅓-yard dark green batik
* Fray Check™

Template

Large diamond template, page 117 (T-3, cut on black lines)

Cutting Plan

From the blue, green, peach, pink, beige, and light green batik, cut:
* 12 diamonds of each (inner and outer diamonds)

From the dark green batik, cut:
* four 2"-wide selvedge-to-selvedge strips (binding)

Assembly

1. Prepare 36 diamonds with the light color inside and the dark on the outside. The combinations are:
   * 12 blue outer/pink inner.
   * 12 green outer/beige inner.
   * 12 peach outer/light green inner.

Assemble the diamond units.

2. Set the peach diamonds so the longer side is horizontal.

3. Cut three peach units in half lengthwise, as shown. These halves will be long and narrow, and they will be used for the top and bottom rows of the quilt.

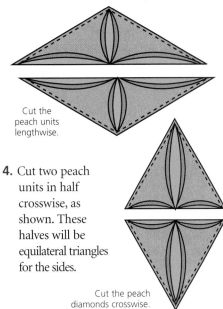

Cut the peach units lengthwise.

4. Cut two peach units in half crosswise, as shown. These halves will be equilateral triangles for the sides.

Cut the peach diamonds crosswise.

5. Stitch together the green and blue diamonds in an alternating row of three green and three blue, as shown.

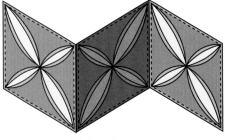

Join the units in rows.

6. Join in rows, inserting peach diamonds and triangles, as shown below.

Join all pieces.

7. Bind, as instructed on pages 16-17.

8. Apply a scant drop of Fray Check deep into the joined corners on the back and front sides of the quilt. Let dry.

9. Toss in the washer and dryer, and fluff.

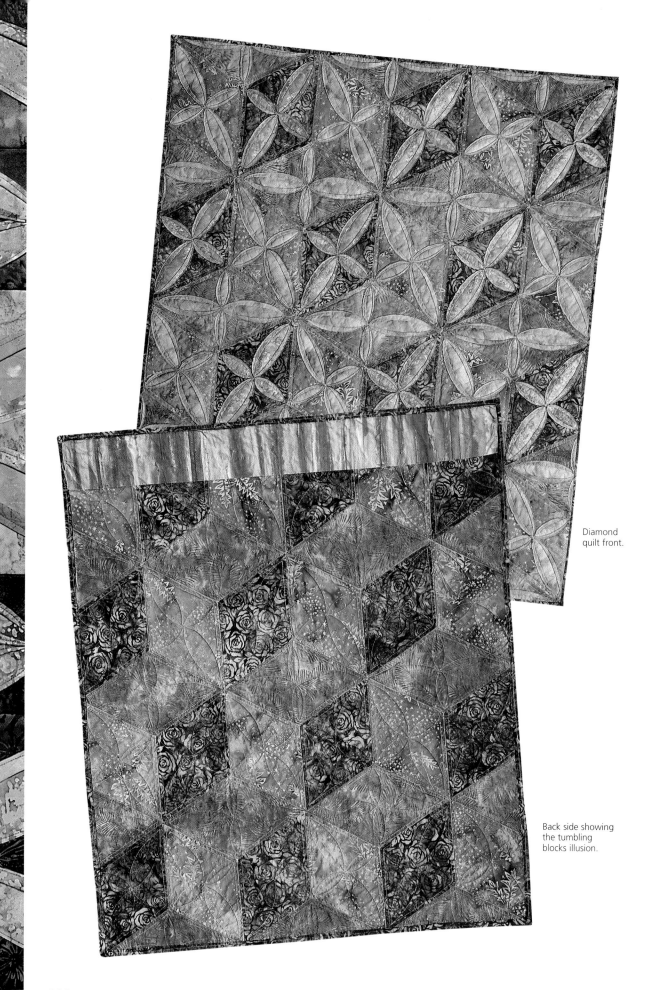

Diamond
quilt front.

Back side showing
the tumbling
blocks illusion.

Square-on-Square Quilt

Bursting with flower petals, this cute design mimics an old-fashioned pattern. It's simple and quick to make, but it looks complicated. The blocks are all cut on the bias; therefore, the fabric fluffs but doesn't shred or string. The fuzzy layers create texture and warmth. It's "quilt-as-you-go."

Finished Size

48" x 60"

Fabric* and Notions

* 3 yards print flannel
* 3 yards plaid homespun
* 3 yards yellow flannel
* 3 yards light green flannel
* ⅓-yard purple flannel
* 1 yard gold flannel
* ⅓-yard dark green flannel
* Fray Check™

*Leave the fabric unlaundered.

Template

None needed. A 9½" square rotary ruler is just the right size.

Cutting Plan

From the print flannel, cut:

* 40 9½" bias squares (outer layer)

From the plaid homespun, cut:

* 40 9½" bias squares (outer layer)

From the yellow flannel, cut:

* 40 9½" bias squares (inner layer)

From the light green flannel, cut:

* 40 9½" bias squares (inner layer)

* Laura's Hint

Cut 9½"-wide diagonal strips (45-degree) from selvedge to selvedge. Crosscut to 9½" squares. At the fold, there is an additional square. Press it open and trim to size.

From the purple flannel, cut:

* 108 2" bias squares (accent squares)

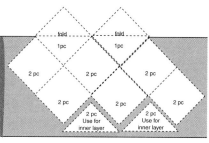

Cutting plan.

From the gold flannel, cut:

* 108 2" bias squares (accent squares)
* eight 1" x 30" bias strips (binding)

From the dark green flannel, cut:

* 108 2" bias squares (accent squares)

* Laura's Hint

Cut each of the accent fabrics into 2"-wide bias strips. Crosscut these strips into 2" bias squares.

Assembly

1. Sort the 9½" bias squares into four groups, as follows:

    * plaid and yellow
    * plaid and green
    * print and yellow
    * print and green

   The plaid and print fabric squares will be the outside layers. The solid colors will be the inside.

2. With right sides out, layer a solid flannel 9½" square on a print 9½" square, matching the corners.

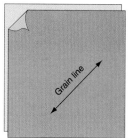

Grain line

Layer the squares.

3. Fold the four corners to the center of the solid square and press.

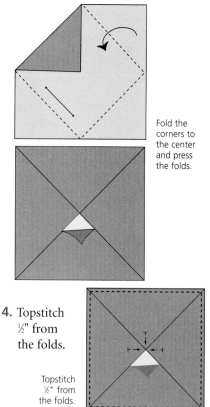

Fold the corners to the center and press the folds.

4. Topstitch ½" from the folds.

Topstitch ½" from the folds.

5. Place four matching accent squares right-side up on top of each folded flap, ¼" from the inner corners, and pin in place.

6. Stitch through the layers in a loopy, flowery design, as shown, catching the accent squares in the stitching.

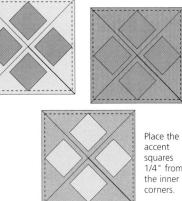

Place the accent squares 1/4" from the inner corners.

Stitch in a flowery pattern.

7. Repeat steps 2 through 6 for the remaining squares.

8. Arrange the squares in 10 rows of eight squares. Alternate the plaid and print outer blocks checkerboard style, while alternating the yellow and green inner blocks. Mix the accent colors evenly as well.

9. Join the squares in pairs along the rows by placing two squares right sides together, matching the corners to be joined.

10. Using a wide zigzag stitch (4mm wide and 1.5mm long) and loosening the upper thread tension one increment, stitch the squares together with an over-edge zigzag. Allow the right swing of the zigzag stitch to fall off the edge of the squares. Back-tack at the beginning and at the end of the seam to secure.

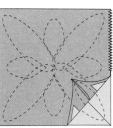

Join the squares with over edge zigzag stitching.

11. Open the joined squares and finger-press the seam open. Repeat for the remaining squares.

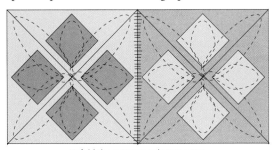

Unfold the squares and press open.

12. With the intersections matched, join the rows using the same zigzag stitch along the seam allowances. Back-tack at the beginning and end.

13. Open the seams and finger-press to flatten.

For the binding:

1. Join the bias binding strips to measure 240".

2. Bind, as instructed on pages 16-17, with the raw edge on the front side of the quilt.

3. Place a drop of Fray Check deep in the corners where the squares meet on the quilt top and on the back to prevent the corners from fraying.

4. Launder the quilt in a warm-water wash with a small amount of detergent. Machine dry.

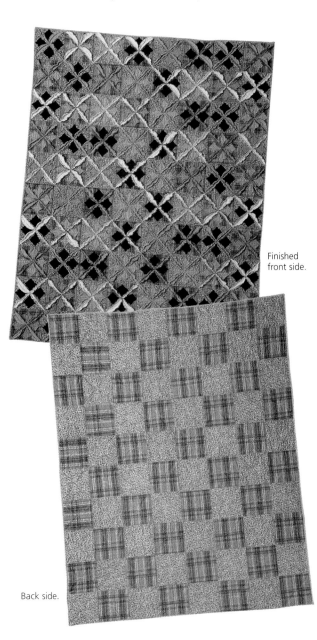

Finished front side.

Back side.

Garden Plants Quilt

C apture the joy of your garden in this quilt. Dimensional leaves surround your flowers with a lovely border. The center flowers burst forth with a spray of petals and points. Use it in your sunroom or liven up a dreary winter corner.

Finished Size

40" square

Fabric and Notions

* 4½ yards tropical print batik
* 1⅔ yards green batik
* ⅝-yard coral batik
* ⅝-yard yellow batik
* ⅝-yard light purple batik
* ⅝-yard dark purple batik
* 1⅓ yards batting

Templates

* Large octagon flower template, page 120 (T-6)
* Octagon batting template, page 121 (T-7, cut on the black lines)

Cutting Plan

From the tropical print, cut:
* eight 21" squares (outside of octagon flowers)
* 18 5" bias squares (10 center patches, four half-square patches, and four corner quarter-square patches)
* five 2"-wide selvedge-to-selvedge strips (binding)
* eight triangles* (outside of leaf units)

From the green batik, cut:
* eight triangles* (inside of leaf units)
* five 2"-wide selvedge-to-selvedge strips (binding)

From the coral batik, cut:
* two 22" squares (octagon flowers)

From the yellow batik, cut:
* two 22" squares (octagon flowers)

From the light purple batik, cut:
* two 22" squares (octagon flowers)

From the dark purple batik, cut:
* two 22" squares (octagon flowers)

From the batting, cut:
* eight octagons (octagon flowers)
* eight 9-3/4" squares (leaf units)
* one 4" x 45" strip crosscut into seven 4" squares (patches)

*Special Triangle Cutting Instructions

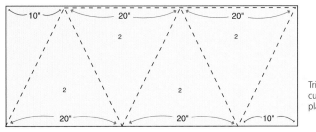

Triangle cutting plan.

1. Cut the folded fabric into two 20" x 50" strips.
2. With a fabric pencil, make a mark every 10" along both long edges.
3. Note the diagram and cut triangles between the marks. There are two layers so each cut will yield two triangles.

Assembly

1. Prepare eight large octagon flower units, as instructed on pages 19-20.
2. Prepare eight basic leaf units, as instructed on page 22.
3. Prepare the patches as listed in the cutting plan, per the instructions on pages 30-31.

(continued)

Assemble the large octagon flower units.

Assemble the basic leaf units.

4. Join the center four large octagon flowers, as shown.

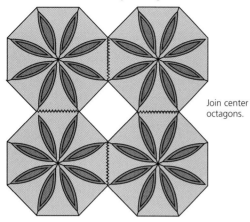

Join center octagons.

5. Stitch the square and half-square patches over the spaces and between the flowers, as shown below.

Insert center patches.

6. Stitch the quarter-square patches to the flower units.

Assemble the flower center.

7. Join four pairs of leaf units (two leaves into four groups), as shown below.

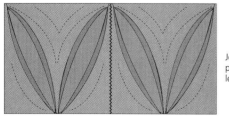

Join the pairs of leaf units.

8. Join one flower unit to each end of two of the leaf groups, as shown below.

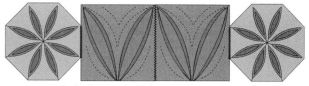

Join the flower units to the ends of the leaf groups.

9. Join the quarter-square patches to the two leaf and flower groups.

10. Join the two leaf groups to the flower center and then join the outer combination rows to the center section, as shown below.

Join the quarter-square patches.

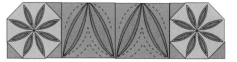

Join the two leaf groups to the flower center.

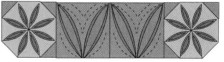

Join the rows.

11. Join the 2" binding strips to measure 184".

12. Bind, as instructed on pages 16-17.

Add the binding.

Larger Garden Quilt

When you need a bigger quilt, increase the center area of the garden quilt by a one row and one column. You'll have nine center flower units that can be made with the same or varied inner fabrics. Make it with shades of yellow and white for a "daisy" feel.

Finished Size

50" square

Fabric and Notions

✳ 7 yards beige batik
✳ ⅜-yard each of seven mixed pink and blue batiks
✳ ⅜-yard each of six mixed green batiks
✳ 2⅓ yards 45"-wide batting

Templates

✳ Large octagon flower template, page 120 (T-6)
✳ Octagon batting template, page 121 (T-7, cut on the black lines)

Cutting Plan

From the beige batik, cut:
✳ 13 22" squares (octagon flowers)
✳ 12 triangles* (leaf units)
✳ 24 5" bias squares (eight center patches, eight half-square patches, and eight quarter-square patches)
✳ six 2" x 40" strips (binding)

From the mixed green batiks, cut:
✳ two triangles of each of the six variations (12 leaf units)

From the mixed pink and blue batiks, cut:
✳ two 22" squares of each fabric (13 octagon flower units plus one extra)

From the batting, cut:
✳ 13 octagons (octagon flowers)
✳ two 4" x 45" strips crosscut into 12 4" squares (patches)
✳ 12 9¾" squares (leaf units)

*Note the special instructions on page 109 for cutting the triangles.
Use two 20" x 70" strips of fabric for 12 triangles.

Assembly

1. Prepare 13 large octagon flower units, as on pages 19-20, and 12 leaf units, as instructed on page 22.

 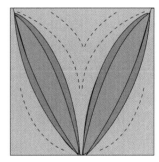

Assemble the octagon flowers and leaf units.

2. Prepare the patches, as listed in the cutting plan, per the instructions on pages 30-31.

3. Join the center nine large octagon flowers.

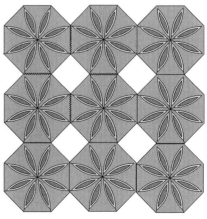

Join center octagons.

4. Stitch the square and half- and quarter-square patches over the spaces and between the flowers, as shown.

5. Join four groups of leaf units (three leaves into four groups).

Insert center and corner patches.

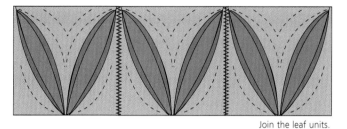

Join the leaf units.

6. Join two flower units to both ends of two of the leaf groups.

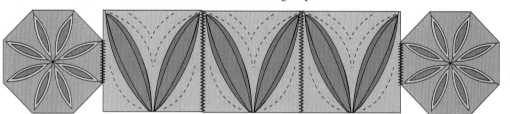

Join the flower units to the leaf groups.

7. Stitch the quarter-square patches to the flower and leaf rows.

8. Join the two three-leaf groups to the flower center.

9. Join the outer combination rows to the center section.

10. Join the 2" binding strips to measure 224".

11. Bind, as instructed on pages 16-17.

Stitch the quarter-square patches to the flower and leaf rows.

Join the three-leaf units to the flower center.

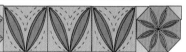

Join the rows.

Add the binding.

Finished quilt.

A Final Word

I hope this book and its projects have brought you pleasure and joy. Share the beauty of nature with your friends and family. Bring warmth with a cozy quilt. Have fun with a cute dimensional bag. Play with fabrics, color, and textures. Experiment and explore—free your creative juices! Teach someone to sew and pass on the skill to a new generation.

Share the creative spirit with a new friend.

For questions, additional information, plastic templates, and other products, contact me at laurafarson@fastfoldedflowers.com or visit my Web site at www.fastfoldedflowers.com.

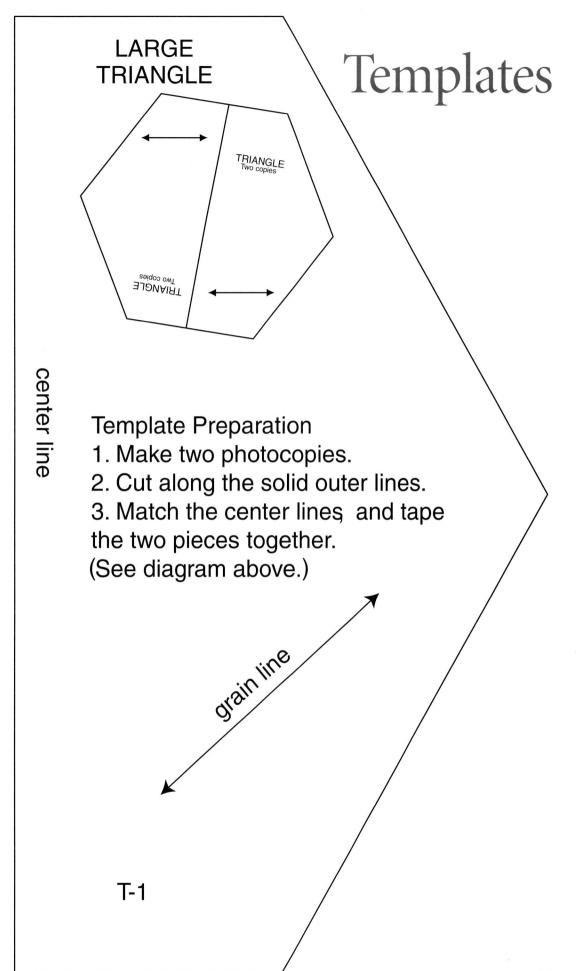

LARGE
TRIANGLE

TRIANGLE
Two copies

TRIANGLE
Two copies

Templates

center line

Template Preparation
1. Make two photocopies.
2. Cut along the solid outer lines.
3. Match the center lines, and tape
the two pieces together.
(See diagram above.)

grain line

T-1

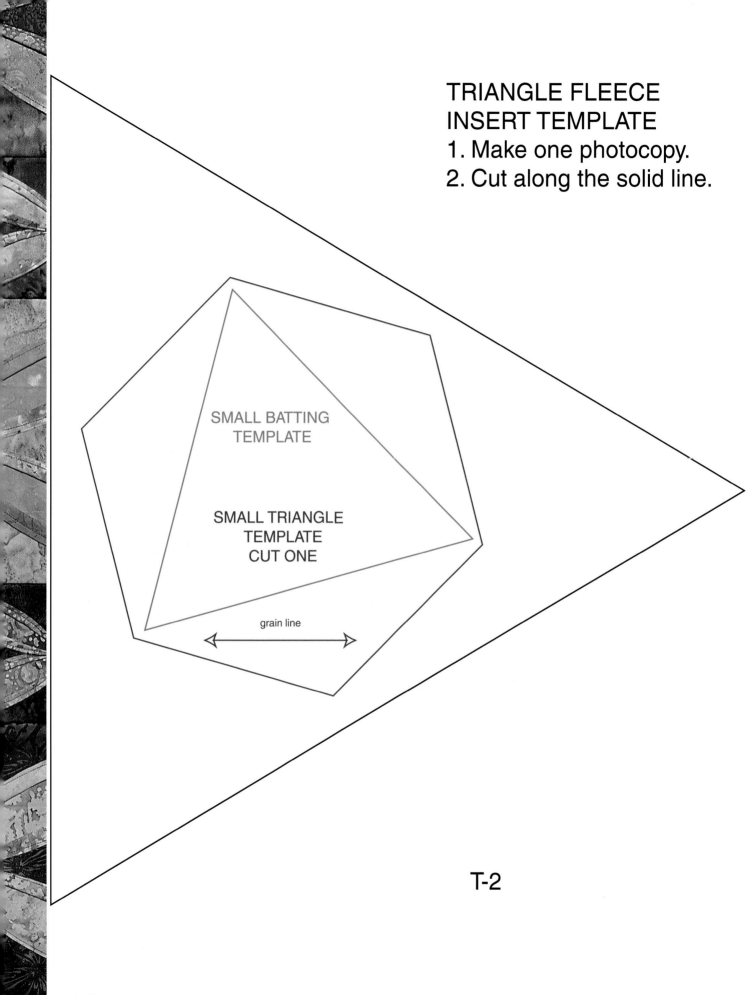

TRIANGLE FLEECE
INSERT TEMPLATE
1. Make one photocopy.
2. Cut along the solid line.

SMALL BATTING
TEMPLATE

SMALL TRIANGLE
TEMPLATE
CUT ONE

grain line

T-2

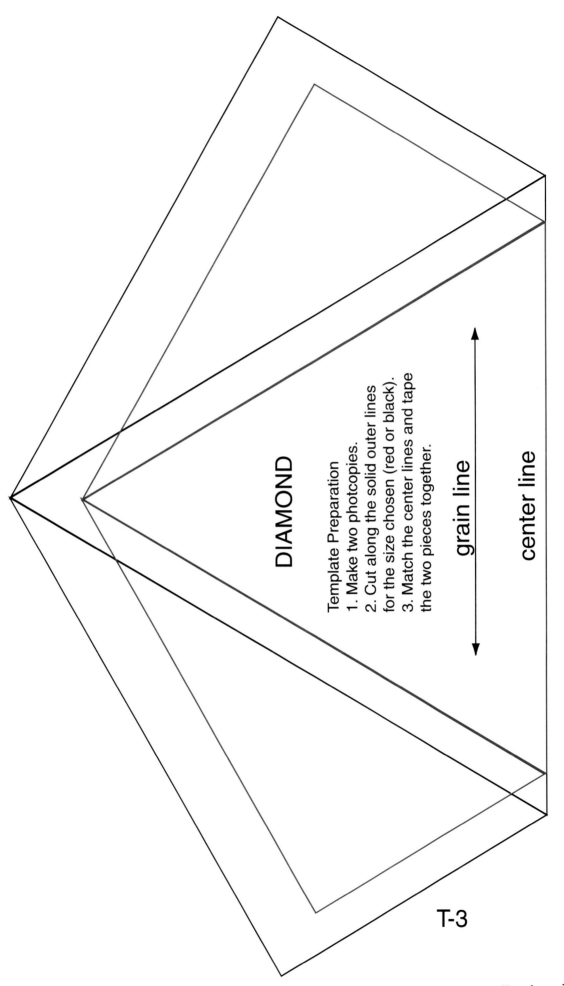

DIAMOND

Template Preparation
1. Make two photcopies.
2. Cut along the solid outer lines
for the size chosen (red or black).
3. Match the center lines and tape
the two pieces together.

grain line

center line

T-3

HEXAGON
Six copies

HEXAGON
Six copies

HEXAGON
Six copies

HEXAGON
Six copies

HEXAGON
Six copies

HEXAGON
Six copies

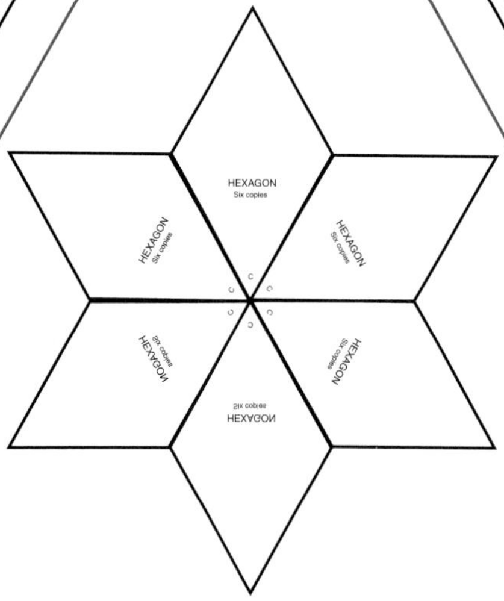

Hexagon Template Preparation
1. Make six photocopies.
2. Cut along the black lines.
3. Tape the diamonds together
three at a time along a
horizontal line.
4. Join the halves together.
(See diagram above.)

HEXAGON
FLOWER

CUT SIX

T-4

C

SMALL DIAMOND
FLEECE TEMPLATE
CUT ONE
on red line

TRIANGLE FOR
JEWEL BOX
Make 2 copies.
Cut on red lines.

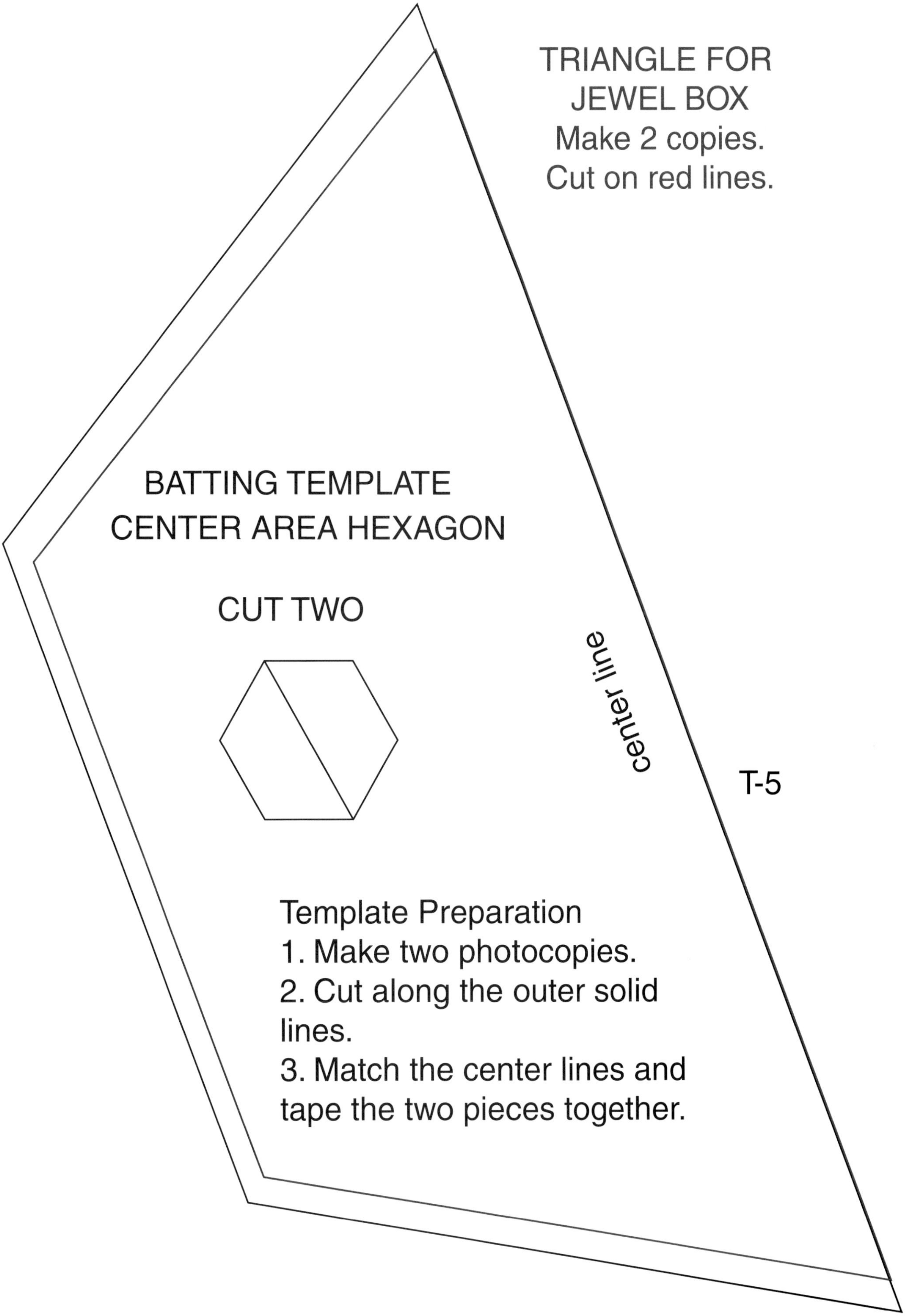

BATTING TEMPLATE
CENTER AREA HEXAGON

CUT TWO

center line

T-5

Template Preparation
1. Make two photocopies.
2. Cut along the outer solid
lines.
3. Match the center lines and
tape the two pieces together.

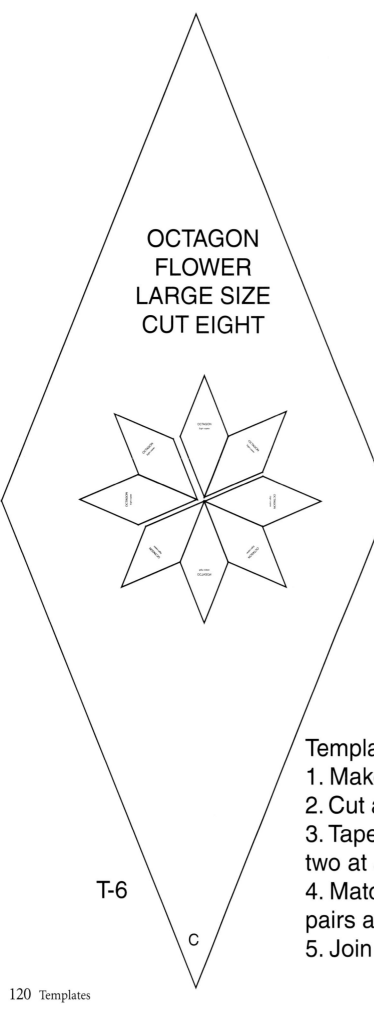

OCTAGON
FLOWER
LARGE SIZE
CUT EIGHT

T-6

C

Template Preparation
1. Make eight photocopies.
2. Cut along the solid outer lines.
3. Tape the diamonds together two at a time.
4. Match the centers and join the pairs along a horizontal line.
5. Join the halves.

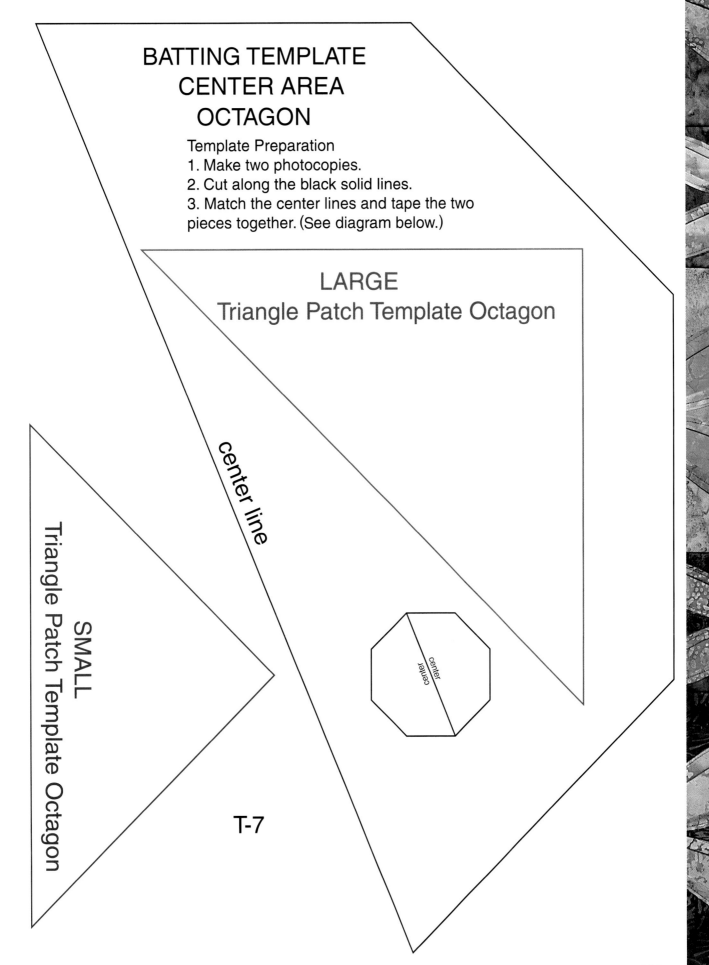

BATTING TEMPLATE
CENTER AREA
OCTAGON

Template Preparation
1. Make two photocopies.
2. Cut along the black solid lines.
3. Match the center lines and tape the two pieces together. (See diagram below.)

LARGE
Triangle Patch Template Octagon

center line

SMALL
Triangle Patch Template Octagon

center
center

T-7

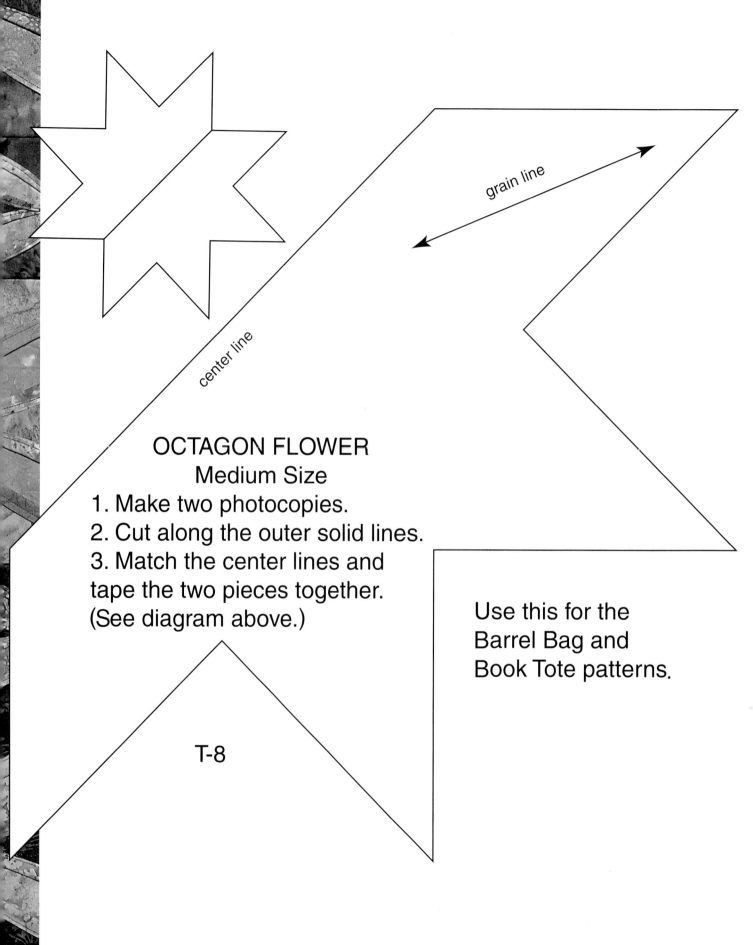

grain line

center line

OCTAGON FLOWER
Medium Size
1. Make two photocopies.
2. Cut along the outer solid lines.
3. Match the center lines and
tape the two pieces together.
(See diagram above.)

Use this for the
Barrel Bag and
Book Tote patterns.

T-8

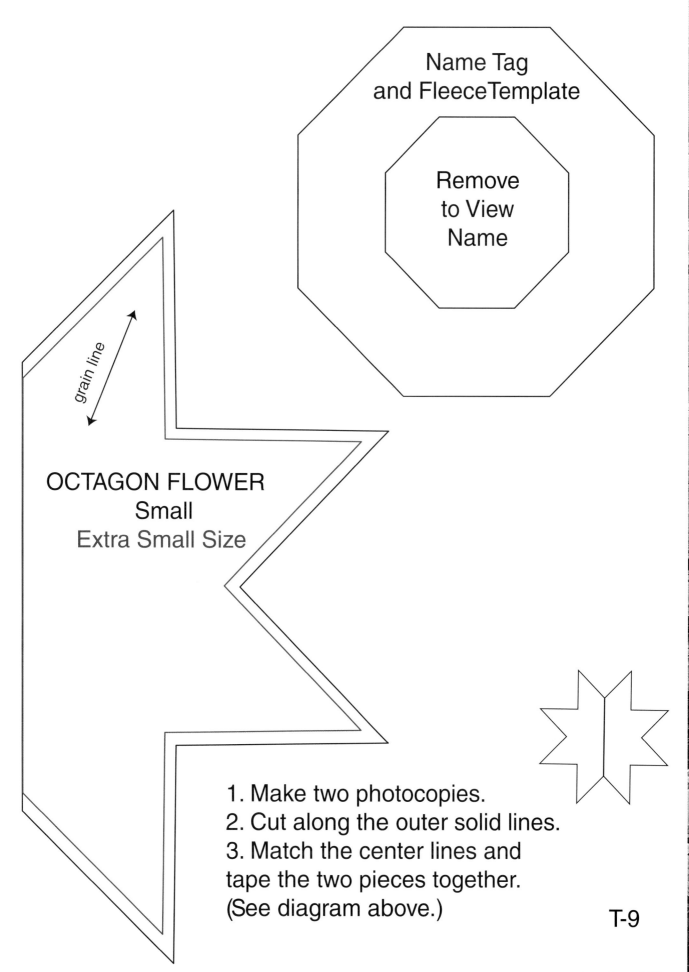

Name Tag
and FleeceTemplate

Remove
to View
Name

grain line

OCTAGON FLOWER
Small
Extra Small Size

1. Make two photocopies.
2. Cut along the outer solid lines.
3. Match the center lines and
tape the two pieces together.
(See diagram above.)

T-9

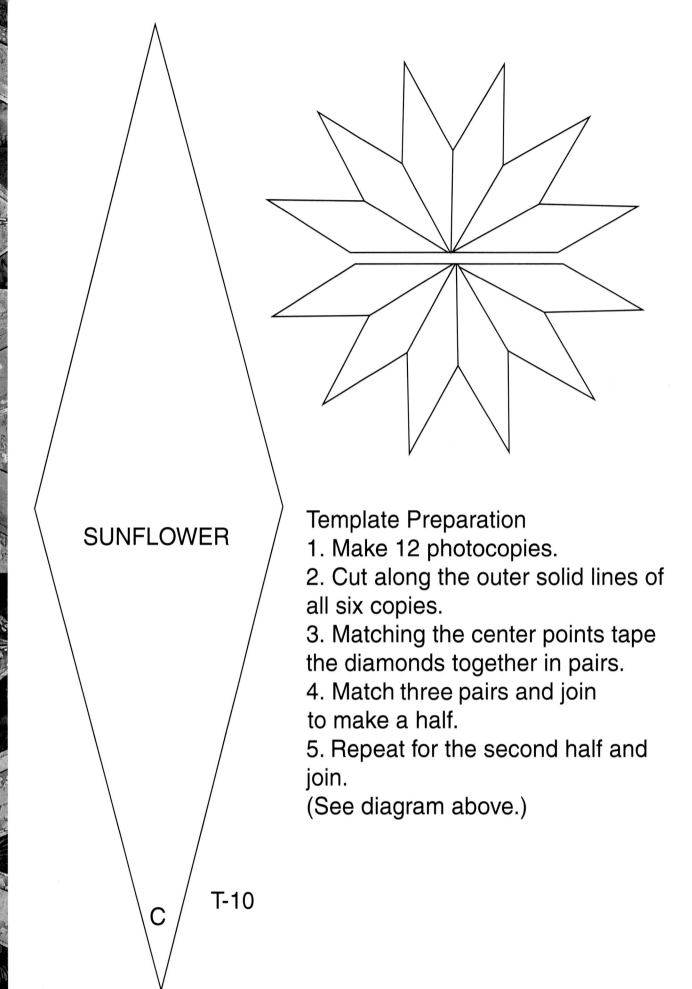

SUNFLOWER

Template Preparation
1. Make 12 photocopies.
2. Cut along the outer solid lines of all six copies.
3. Matching the center points tape the diamonds together in pairs.
4. Match three pairs and join to make a half.
5. Repeat for the second half and join.
(See diagram above.)

C

T-10

Template Preparation
1. Make two photocopies.
2. Cut along the outer solid lines.
3. Match the center lines and tape the two pieces together.

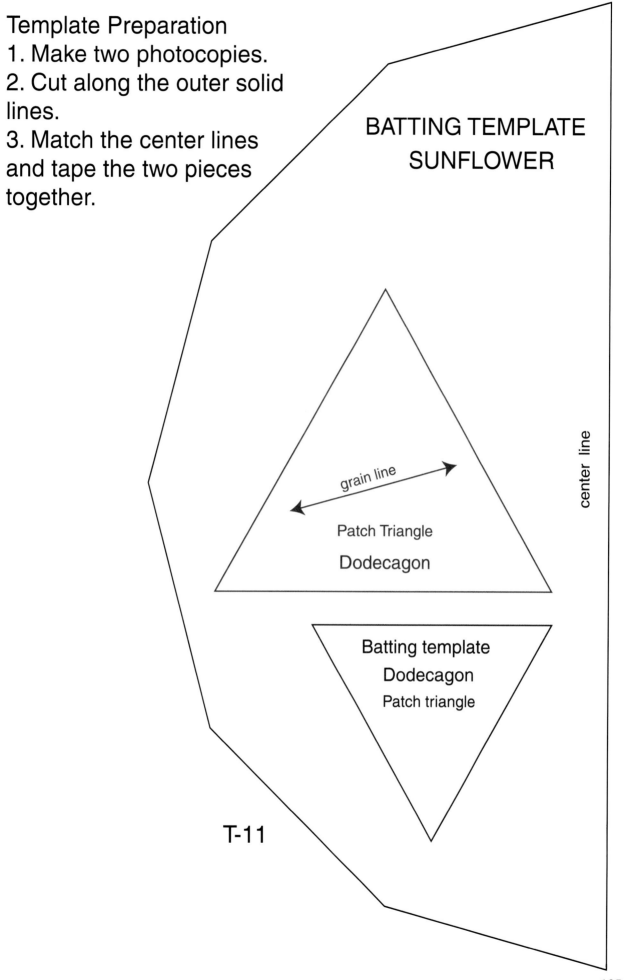

BATTING TEMPLATE
SUNFLOWER

grain line

Patch Triangle

Dodecagon

center line

Batting template

Dodecagon

Patch triangle

T-11

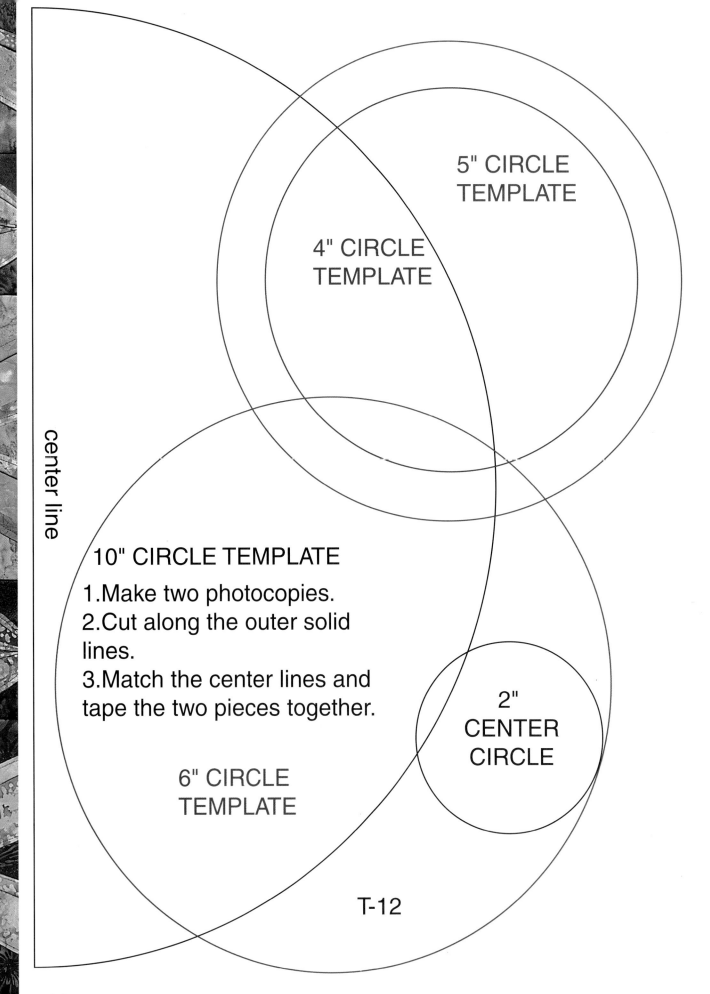

5" CIRCLE
TEMPLATE

4" CIRCLE
TEMPLATE

10" CIRCLE TEMPLATE

1. Make two photocopies.
2. Cut along the outer solid lines.
3. Match the center lines and tape the two pieces together.

6" CIRCLE
TEMPLATE

2"
CENTER
CIRCLE

T-12

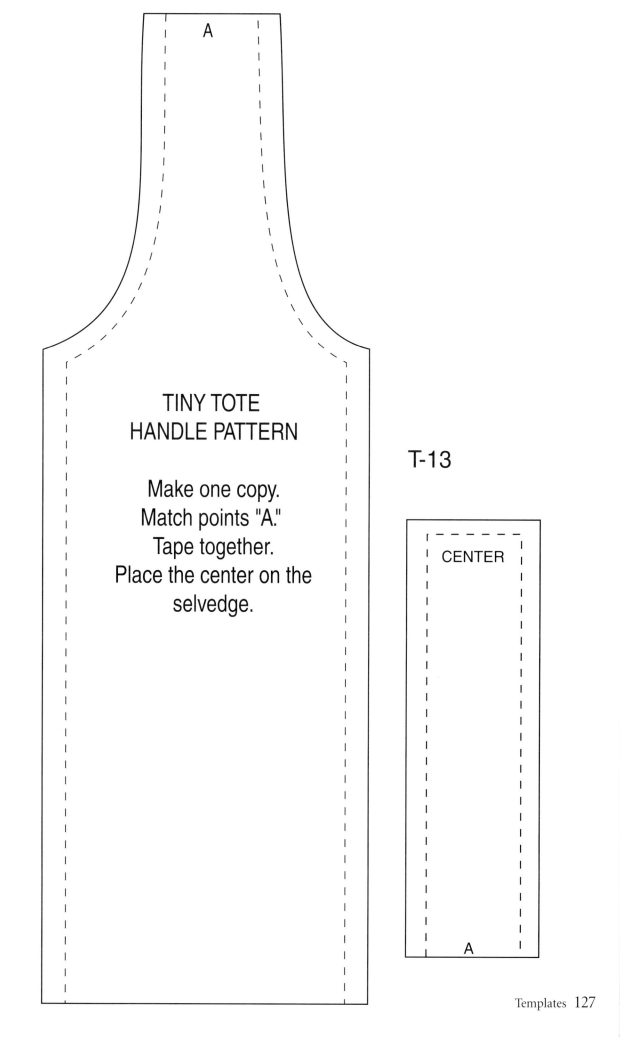

A

TINY TOTE
HANDLE PATTERN

Make one copy.
Match points "A."
Tape together.
Place the center on the
selvedge.

T-13

CENTER

A

Fresh Ideas & NEW TECHNIQUES for Quilters

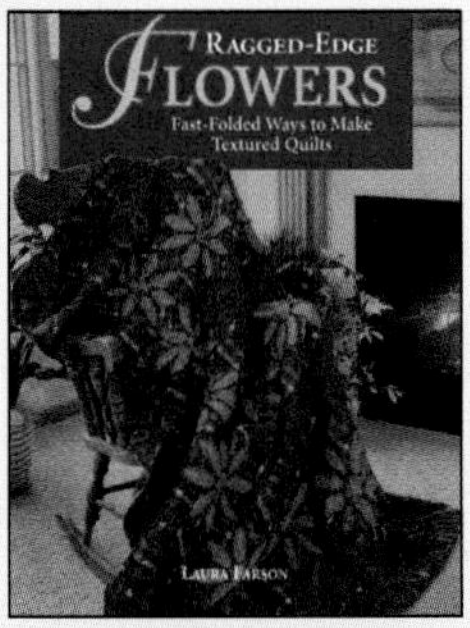

Ragged-Edge Flowers
Fast-Folded Ways to Make Textured Quilts
by Laura Farson

It's fast, fun, and easy to create ragged-edge floral quilts with Laura Farson's timesaving technique! You'll find more than 12 unique patterns for quilted wall hangings, pillow covers, and quilts. Instructions are easy-to-follow and the minimal sewing and "quilt-as-you-go" method makes these 18 projects attainable for any skill level.

Softcover • 8¼ x 10⅞ • 96 pages
150+ color photos
Item# REF • $19.95

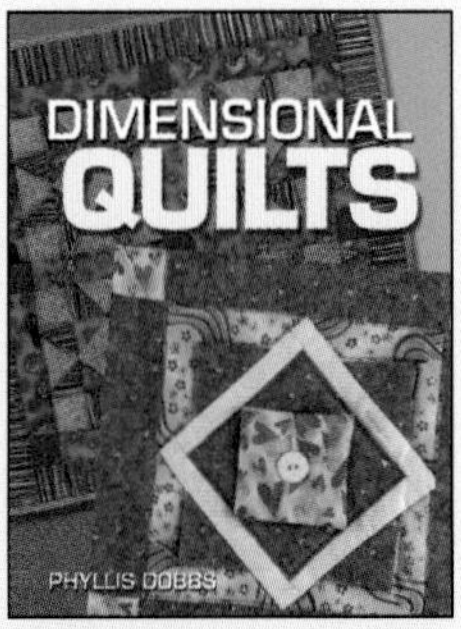

Dimensional Quilts
by Phyllis Dobbs

Create a dimensional quilt that really stands out in the crowd with this incredibly easy technique! You'll learn how to use batting to increase the thickness of certain pieces and then follow special stitching instructions for a dramatic dimensional effect. Easily apply this new technique through step-by-step instructions to more than 25 projects, such as placemats, window valances, photo album covers, pillows, and a variety of holiday decorations. Whether you're a new or experienced sewer, you'll love these fresh quilting ideas.

Softcover • 8¼ x 10⅞• 128 pages
125 color photos
Item# DIMQL • $21.99

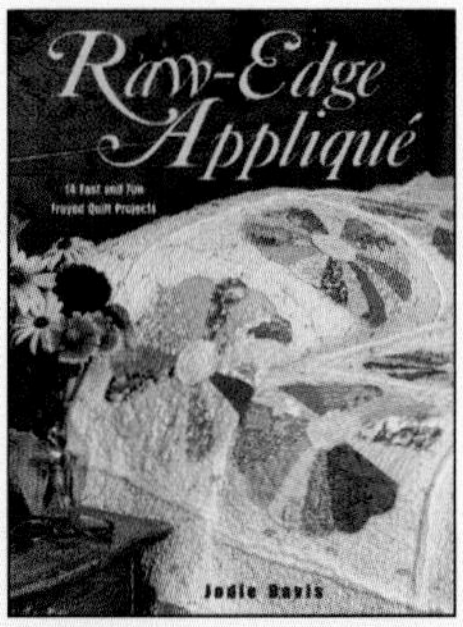

Raw Edge Appliqué
by Jodie Davis

Imagine making a Dresden Plate minus fussy needle-turn appliqué or an Orange Peel without matching a curve— sound like a dream? Well, with Jodie Davis' new book, it's a reality! You'll find 10 fun and fast quilt projects that eliminate hours of pinning and matching by using a straight machine stitch. The raw edges are left exposed to become slightly frayed as the quilt is loved, washed and dried-and then loved some more. Features easy-to-follow instructions, detailed illustrations and gorgeous photos of the finished quilts.

Softcover • 8¼ x 10⅞ • 96 pages
20 color photos
Item# FEQ • $19.95

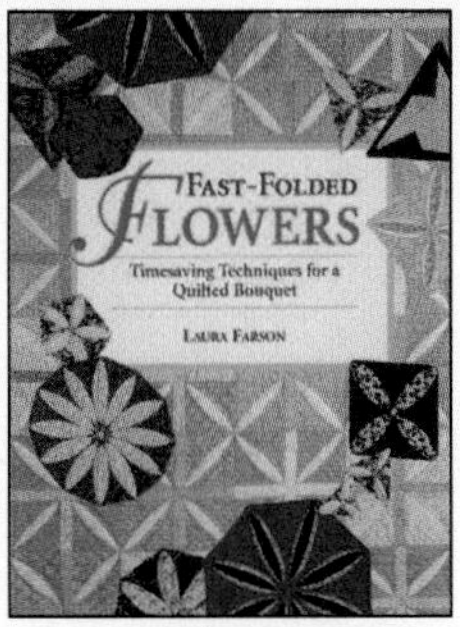

Fast-Folded Flowers
Timesaving Techniques for a Quilted Bouquet
by Laura Farson

Who can resist a bouquet of beautiful flowers, especially when they're three-dimensional quilted designs? Learn 12 quick and easy techniques for flower petal quilt blocks that can be used to create quilts, lap robes, baby blankets, trivet covers, potholders, and home décor items. Easy to understand instructions for 17 projects that utilize a sewing machine and no handwork offer quick, eye-appealing results. Quilters, crafters, and sewers of all skill levels will enjoy creating these delightful quilted bouquets.

Softcover • 8¼ x 10⅞ • 128 pages
175 color photos & illus.
Item# FFFQT • $21.95

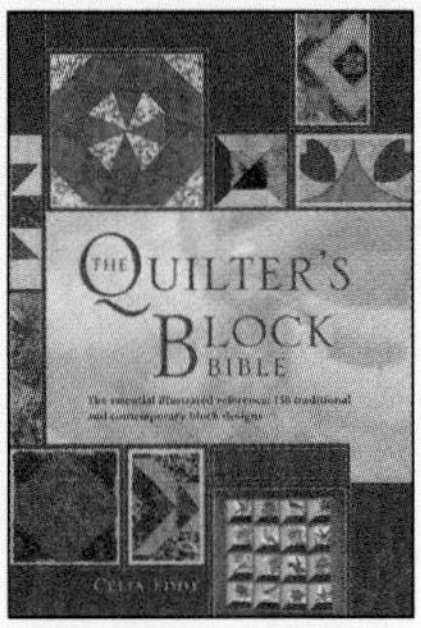

The Quilter's Block Bible
by Celia Eddy

Create more than 100 individual quilt blocks and receive expert tips and techniques for creating your own quilt blocks in this spiral-bound guide. Learn how quilt blocks are categorized and follow selected examples from different categories to draft, design, and create custom patchwork. You'll receive great ideas, hints, and tips on layout, colors, and fabrics. Each block entry includes a photograph of the finished block, diagrams, and instructions for clear guidance.

Hardcover w/Concealed Spiral • 5¾ x 7¾
256 pages • 150 color photos
Item# QBB • $29.99

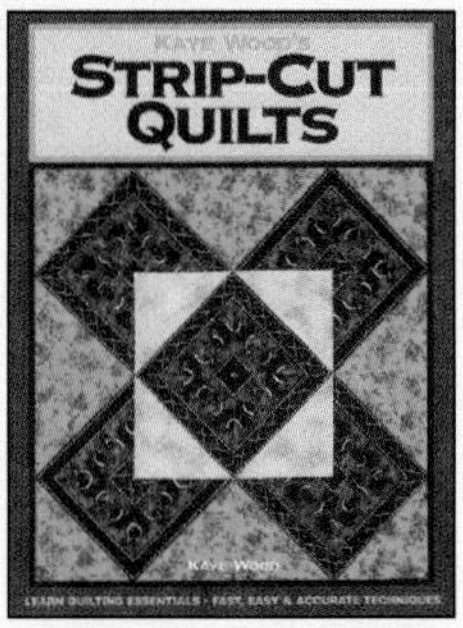

Kaye Wood's Strip-Cut Quilts
by Kaye Wood

Learn timesaving techniques for accurate cutting and quilting with renowned quilter Kaye Wood. Explore the many triangle shapes that can be cut with the Starmaker® 8 Master Template including horizontal and vertical cuts, fussy cuts, flying geese, trees and many more. Use these shapes to create 25 beautiful projects including quilts, wall hangings, and table runners. Both beginning and advanced quilters will love Kaye Wood's easy strip-cutting techniques.

Softcover • 8¼ x 10⅞ • 96 pages
200 illus. • 30 color photos
Item# KWNSQ • $19.95

kp krause publications Offer CRB4

P.O. Box 5009, Iola WI 54945-5009 • www.krausebooks.com

To order call **(800) 258-0929** Offer CRB4

Please add $4.00 for the first book and $2.25 each additional for shipping and handling to U.S. addresses. Non-U.S. addresses please add $20.95 for the first book and $5.95 each additional. Residents of CA, IA, IL, KS, NJ, PA, SD, TN, and WI, please add appropriate sales tax.